OF THESE YE MAY FREELY EAT

A VEGETARIAN COOKBOOK

by

JoAnn Rachor

Published by
FAMILY HEALTH PUBLICATIONS L. L. C.
8777 E. Musgrove Hwy
Sunfield MI 48890

Table of Contents

FROM THE AUTHOR

I was a compulsive overeater. I had no concern about what I ate, drank, or smoked until one night in a college class. It was 1973 during my sophomore year at Central Michigan University. I was taking a class that did not apply to my major, as one of my electives, because it looked like easy credit. My teacher took an interest in the students, and was an inspiration to me. One evening she presented some material about vegetarianism. This caught my attention, and for the first time in my life I really wanted to study something. I scoured the library for everything I could read on the subject. Within days I decided to make a change that had never before crossed my mind. I began eating vegetables, salads, and peanut butter lettuce sandwiches. I became interested in nutrition and soon changed my major to Home Economics with an emphasis in Nutrition.

My parents were surprised and had a lot of questions about my new vegetarianism, but they could see I was doing my homework. They became very supportive. When I went home for the summer they worked hard to help me plant my very first garden. It was big and beautiful with all kinds of vegetables and flowers. Mom and I bought cookbooks. We did lots of experimenting with foods we had never before eaten. I can remember, like yesterday (it has been 26 years as I write this), making guacamole with an unripe avocado, a taste impossible to describe or to forget. I can still clearly remember my dear parents sitting at the table on many days that summer being very willing guinea pigs as we tried recipes. Unfortunately, I can't remember very many of them turning out too well, but you have to start somewhere. I am thankful and glad I started in my family's kitchen. They still support and encourage me and are willing to try anything I make at least once. Over time, my parents dramatically changed their eating habits also as they saw the value of a vegetarian diet.

In 1978 I was excited for the opportunity to get unique and extremely valuable training which has enabled me to help hundreds of people. For two years I studied and worked under Doctors Calvin and Agatha Thrash and their trained staff. The Thrashes are the founders of Uchee Pines Institute, located in East Central Alabama, 15 miles from Columbus, Georgia. The institute has a Lifestyle counseling program for individuals, like myself, who wish to understand how to use natural remedies and lifestyle changes in the prevention and treatment of disease. It also operates a small health-conditioning center for up to 14 patients. Most that come for treatment suffer from chronic diseases such as heart disease, diabetes, high blood pressure, and obesity. I never cease to be amazed at how wonderfully God has created our bodies, and how they respond so dramatically to the use of natural remedies. If you would like to learn how you can receive this practical training or go for patient care, write: Uchee Pines Institute, 30 Uchee Pines Rd, Seale, AL 36875-5702 or call 334-855-4781.

In 1981 my father, at age 59, was a picture of health. However, he began experiencing chest pain as he would walk the hills on their property. After failing a stress test and having a heart catheterization he was found to have two arteries 60%, one 80%, and two 95% narrowed. With too many years of too much fat, too much stress and too little heart-strengthening exercise, it was recommended he undergo an immediate quadruple bypass. He was in serious condition; but dad decided to take another route. He believed in what I had learned at Uchee Pines, and had begun changing his diet towards vegetarianism a year or two earlier. Now, with this diagnosis, he became even more careful about what he ate. Gradually, he developed an exercise program of walking and swimming. Today, at age 76, he is very physically active, and in my observation, has the strength and endurance of a healthy man half his age.

I have met many people who want to make improvements in their lifestyles. What would I advise someone who is in the early stages of making changes for the better? Educate yourself and those you hope to influence with books, videos, and other tools. Find ways to explain, in a positive, interesting way, what you would like to do. One year my mom gave a talk and won her kindergarten class over to using carob milk instead of chocolate milk. She asked how many liked it, and they were all enthusiastic. The next day she was fixing them carob milk again, and a boy was there who missed the previous day's pep talk. Needless to say, he wasn't very willing to try something new, and stated his dislike for the drink. Along with education, I suggest making gradual changes. Sometimes it is good to start with drinking more water between meals, or increasing whole grains in the diet, such as popcorn without butter, oats, or whole grain breads. For others, a good place to begin is getting more exercise or going to bed earlier.

These simple laws of health may seem confining, but as one who has suffered and has experienced the consequences of intemperance, I can say with all my heart, they really are an INESTIMABLE BLESSING!

WORDS FOUND IN "CAPITAL LETTERS"

You will find words in some of the recipes in CAPITAL LETTERS. This is to direct you to look up that word in the index at the back of the book. This refers either to a recipe that is being used within a recipe OR to a define an ingredient.

The following words that need to be defined are:

NUTS AND SEEDS:

Nuts and seeds are interchangeable in these recipes. Nuts that are most versatile are raw cashews and almonds because of their mild flavor and light color. If almonds still have their skin on then they will leave brown flecks if the product is blended to a cream. If this is undesirable than blanch the almonds. (To do this drop whole almonds into boiling water for not more than one minute or they will discolor. Pour into a colander and rinse under cold water. Drain. Pop off skins and discard.) Raw sunflower seeds are economical. They are not quite as mild in flavor as cashews and almonds nor are they quite as light in color so the recipe will be a shade darker but they are very exceptable to use. They are an advantage to use if recipe calls for chopped nuts as sunflower seeds need no chopping. Other nuts, such as, walnuts, pecans and brazil nuts are delicious in many recipes but because of their strong flavor it is usually best to leave them out of cheeses, dressings and spreads. Nuts supply tenderness and flavor, often in place of oil.

SWEETENER:

Recipes calling for SWEETENER are flexible and will turn out good whether using a liquid or dry sweetening agent. Honey, brown rice syrup, cane sugar crystals, corn syrup, brown or white sugar may be used. Use your preference or what is on hand.

YEAST FLAKES:

Not the same as baking yeast used for raising bread. Yeast flakes are sold under names such as nutritional yeast flakes, food yeast, Red Star nutritional yeast and yeast flakes. Most Brewers Yeast has a strong flavor and will not taste good in recipes. If the nutritional yeast is in a powdered form use about 2/3 of what is called for in the cheese and spread recipes in this book. Do not bother changing the amount of yeast called for in the entrees if using powdered yeast.

CRACKERS AND BREADS

The following crackers and breads are made without baking powder or baking soda. These items leave residues in the breads that injure the body, or they damage the grains during the cooking process, making breads less nourishing.

OAT CRACKERS

1 1/2 cups quick oats
1 cup whole grain flour
1/2 cup wheat germ or bran

1/2 teaspoon salt
1/3 cup oil
2/3 cup water

Mix dry and wet ingredients separately, then combine together. Roll out 1/8 inch thick onto an oiled 11x15 cookie sheet. Score. Bake at 325 degrees for 20-25 minutes.

BREAD STICKS

2 cups quick or rolled oats
1/2 cup whole grain flour
2 teaspoons SWEETENER pg 6

1 teaspoon salt
3/4 cup NUTS OR SEEDS pg 6
2/3 cup water

Blend oats until a flour. Remove from blender. Blend water, sweetener, salt and nuts or seeds of your choice until smooth. Stir together all ingredients. Pinch off 1 tablespoon of dough. Roll between hands to make a stick 2-3 inches long. Bake on oiled cookie sheet at 350 degrees for 25 minutes.

CRACKERS: Roll out on oiled 11x15 cookie sheet. Bake at 350 degrees for 15 to 20 minutes.
PIE CRUST: This dough will cover 2-9 inch oiled pie plates. Bake at 350 degrees for 15 to 20 minutes.

SOY CORN MUFFINS

2 cups soaked soybeans
2 cups water
2 tablespoons SWEETENER pg 6

2 cups cornmeal
2 teaspoons salt
1/4 cup quick or rolled oats

Soak dry soy beans in plenty of water 6-8 hours (1 cup dry equals about 2 1/4 cups soaked). Drain. Blend smooth all but cornmeal, stir in cornmeal. Filled oiled muffin tins or cast iron gem pans. Bake at 375 for 45 minutes.

TIPS FOR BAKING YEAST BREADS

INGREDIENTS:

A. Flour- The higher gluten content of hard wheat flour, in comparison to soft wheat or pastry flour, is the best for baking bread. A mixture of two or three different kinds of flour can be quite nutritious. Most other kinds of flour have a low gluten content in them. Therefore, they should be limited to about one fifth of the total flour in the recipe. Soy flour adds moistness to a loaf. Keep flour in a cool place for long storage.

B. Yeast- Baking yeast may be purchased prepackaged in one tablespoon proportions. It may also be obtained by bulk in 1/4 to 1 pound packages or more. The savings of buying in bulk can be tremendous. Yeast should be stored in the refrigerator or freezer. It will remain fresh for months or even more than a year with proper storage. Freshness may be tested by adding room temperature yeast to warm water and a small amount of sweetener or as the recipe calls for. If it bubbles and foams within five to ten minutes the yeast is still active. Yeast also comes in instant form.

C. Sweetener- The main purpose of sweetener in bread is to feed or help develop the yeast. Sweeteners, such as honey, molasses and sugar will accomplish this, as well as fruit juice and fruit sauce.

D. Salt- 1 teaspoon per 2 1/2 - 3 cups of flour is a general amount used.

E. Fat- This helps to provide tenderness and moistness. Bread can be quite acceptable without added fat. The key is not using too much flour. Stop adding flour when dough is still slightly sticky but can be kneaded. Soy flour or ground nuts also add moistness.

F. Water Temperature- Yeast develops best if the water it is added to is 85-100 degrees.

COMBINING INGREDIENTS:

A. Order- First stir together warm water, sweetener and yeast, let sit 5- 10 minutes while yeast bubbles and foams. Then add salt, oil and half of the wheat flour. Develop the gluten in the batter by vigorously stirring 1-2 minutes, then add remaining flour.

B. Kneading- This develops more gluten. It is done by rolling, folding and pushing of the dough with the hands for about 5 minutes. To prevent dough from sticking to hands either moisten hands and kneading surface with a little water or lightly flour hands and kneading surface.

C. Raising- This helps to lighten the bread. After kneading cover the dough with a clean towel and let double in bulk. This takes 30-45 minutes. Then the dough is punched down and kneaded for 3-4 minutes. If the dough is allowed to raise 1 or 2 times before placing in the bread pan it will increase in lightness.

D. Preparation of Pans- Sometimes just using oil on pans is not sufficient to keep bread from sticking. Food release sprays, such as Pam, work very well or make your own by mixing 1 part liquid lecithin with 6 parts vegetable oil. Store in a glass jar. Wipe with paper towel or use a pastry brush to oil pans.

E. Shaping into Pan- Press out dough either with a rolling pin or hands to remove air bubbles. Roll or form the dough into a smooth loaf. Tuck it in so that the edges touch the sides of the pan. Cover the pan with a towel. When dough is doubled in bulk and ready to bake a slight indentation made with the finger will remain rather than spring back. If in doubt it is better to be slightly under raised as over raised dough will fall during baking. Place pans in preheated oven.

BAKING, EATING AND STORING:

A. Time and Temperature- The temperature is usually 350 degrees. The time depends on the size of the loaf. A one pound loaf bakes in 35-40 minutes. A two pound loaf in 45-50 minutes.

B. Check for Doneness- Particularly if not using oil it is important not to over bake bread. This causes dryness. The bread is done if it slips easily from a properly oiled pan and the hand can be placed on the bottom of the loaf without burning. Remove bread from pans immediately and place on racks to cool. Cover with a towel while cooling.

C. Bagging and Storage- Let bread cool before bagging. It should feel cool and dry to the touch. Bread keeps several weeks in the freezer, several days in the refrigerator and few days at room temperature.

D. When to Eat- While bread dough is rising and baking there are some volatile substances left in the bread after the fermentation process of the yeast has taken place. These substances evaporate in 2-3 days. Yeast bread in more healthful and digestible after this waiting period. The conditioning of the bread also improves during this time, making the bread easier to cut.

TROUBLE SHOOTING FOR BAKING YEAST BREADS

1. SOUR TASTE
   a. Water too warm.
   b. Period of rising too long. Do not expect whole grain breads to rise as high as white breads.
   c. Temperature too high while rising.
   d. Poor yeast.

2. DRY OR CRUMBLY
   a. Too much flour in dough.
   b. Over-baking.
   c. Using flour with low gluten content. Hard spring or winter wheat is best for baking.

3. HEAVINESS
   a. Unevenness of temperature while rising.
   b. Insufficient kneading.
   c. Old flour.
   d. Old yeast.

4. CRACKS IN CRUST
   a. Baking before sufficiently raised.

5. DARK PATCHES OR STREAKS
   a. Mix shortening into liquid before adding flour, thus avoiding flour from becoming coated with fat before it has mixed evenly with the liquid.

6. SOGGINESS
   a. Too much liquid.
   b. Insufficient baking.
   c. Bagging before bread has completely cooled.

7. ILL-SHAPED LOAF
   a. Not formed well originally when made into a loaf.
   b. Rising period too long then loaf falls while baking.
   c. Flat on top may be from inadequate kneading.

8. HOLES IN BREAD
   a. From not getting all the air bubbles out when kneading the second time after the dough has risen in the bowl. Knead more thoroughly.

BASIC WHOLE WHEAT BREAD

1 cup warm water
1 tablespoon SWEETENER pg 6
1 tablespoon yeast

1 teaspoon salt
1 tablespoon oil
3 cups whole wheat flour

Dissolve sweetener in the water then stir in yeast. Let stand 5-8 minutes as the yeast begins to bubble. Stir in the oil and salt. Add 1 1/2 cups flour. Beat vigorously for 1 minute. Add remaining flour gradually. Use only the amount of flour necessary to handle dough without it sticking to your hands. Lightly flour table and knead dough 5 minutes. Add more flour if necessary. Place dough in a large bowl, cover with a clean towel. Let dough rise until double, 30-45 minutes. Punch down, knead briefly. Squeeze out all air bubbles. Shape into loaf. Place in a medium size oiled loaf pan. Cover with a towel. Let rise until nearly double in size, 30-45 minutes. Bake at 350 degrees for 35-40 minutes, until golden brown and bread slips from the pan. Cool on a rack. See **TIPS FOR BAKING YEAST BREADS** for more help.

VARIATIONS:
1. For a lighter loaf substitute 1/4 cup gluten flour for 1/4 cup of the ww flour. Or use 1 cup of white flour in place of 1 cup of ww flour.
2 .Leave out the oil and use 1/2 cup soy flour. Use less ww flour.
3. For a PIZZA crust, APPLE ICING crust or POT PIE crust. Reduce yeast to 1 teaspoon. When making one of these crusts try using all whole wheat pastry flour instead of regular ww flour. The crust will be more tender.

WHOLE WHEAT BREAD OR BURGER BUNS

3 cups warm water
2 tablespoons SWEETENER pg 6
1 1/2 tablespoons yeast

1 tablespoon salt
1/4 cup oil
8-9 cups whole wheat flour

Follow mixing directions for BASIC WHOLE WHEAT BREAD. This recipe will make 3 one pound loaves or 2 large loaves. For buns divide dough into 18-20 pieces. Shape into balls then slightly flatten by pressing between palms. Place on oiled cookie sheets, not quite touching. Let rise 20 minutes or until almost double in size. Bake at 350 degrees for 25-30 minutes, until golden brown.

VARIATIONS:
1. For lighter bread replace 3 cups of whole wheat flour with 3 cups of white flour.
2. Or, for a lighter loaf replace 1 cup of whole wheat flour with 1 cup of

gluten flour.

3. Leave out oil. Replace 1 1/4 cups whole wheat flour with 1 1/4 cups soy flour. Soy flour increases moistness of bread.

4. Or replace the oil with 2/3 cup apple sauce. Approximately 1 cup of additional flour will be needed (only add enough to be able to knead the dough, too much flour will make the loaf more dry). Over baking will also dry out the bread.

DILLY BREAD

2 cups chopped onions	**3 tablespoons oil**
1/2 cup water	**1/3 cup YEAST FLAKES pg 6**
3 cup warm water	**1/4 cup dill weed OR**
1/4 cup SWEETENER pg 6	**3 tablespoon ground dill seed**
1 tablespoon yeast	**3 cups white flour**
1 tablespoon salt	**7-8 cups whole wheat flour**

Cook onions in the 1/2 cup water. Combine sweetener, yeast and warm water, let stand a few minutes until bubbles appear. Add 4 cups of flour to the yeast mixture. Stir vigorously about 1 minute. Stir in all remaining ingredients except the remaining flour. After this is well mixed start gradually mixing in the flour until the dough is slightly sticky but does not stick to hands. Cover dough with a towel. Let rise until double in size. Punch down, knead and form into loaves. Place in 3 oiled pans. Let rise until almost double, 30-45 minutes. Bake at 350 degrees for 35-40 minutes.

ZWIEBACK

Translated from German to English zwieback means "twice baked". This bread is easier to digest than if bread were not toasted at all. Use any kind of yeast bread except cracked wheat. Lay bread slices on oven rack. Bake at 200 degrees for 1 1/2-2 1/2 hours until crispy dry. Some bread dries faster due to lightness or thinness. Watch for burning. If using a gas oven the pilot light may be sufficient to dry bread overnight.

CROUTONS

Follow directions for zwieback but first cut bread in cubes before drying on a cookie sheet. May even want to experiment with putting some seasonings such as onion and garlic powder, herbs, seasoned salt and yeast flakes in a plastic bag or large bowl. Shake or stir the cubed bread then spread on a cookie sheet.

DROP BISCUITS

1 cup warm water
1 tablespoon SWEETENER pg 6
1 tablespoon yeast
1 1/2 cups whole wheat flour

2/3 cup quick or rolled oats
3/4 teaspoon salt
1/2 cup NUTS OR SEEDS pg 6
1/2 cup water

Combine first three ingredients and let stand about 5-8 minutes, until yeast bubbles. Blend oats to make a flour then empty into a bowl. Blend nuts or seeds and remaining water until smooth. Stir together well all ingredients. Drop by large spoonfuls onto oiled cookie sheet. Let rise 10 minutes. Bake at 350 degrees for 25-30 minutes. Makes 15.

BASIC WHOLE WHEAT MUFFIN MIX

2 cups warm water
2 tablespoons honey
1 1/2 tablespoons yeast

1 1/2 teaspoons salt
3 cups whole wheat flour
1/2 cup white flour
2 tablespoons oil

Combine first three ingredients and let stand about 5-8 minutes, until yeast bubbles. Then stir in well remaining ingredients. Oil muffins tins. Fill 3/4 full with batter. Let rise 10 minutes. Bake at 350 degrees for 30-35 minutes. Makes 12-18

BASIC BISCUITS

Drop by large spoonfuls onto oiled cookie sheet. Let rise 10 minutes. Bake at 350 degrees for 25-30 minutes.

BASIC BATTER BREAD

Fill oiled mini bread pans, 3/4 full, let rise 10 minutes. Bake at 350 degrees for 35 minutes. Each recipe will fill 2 or 3 pans depending on the pan size.

VARIATIONS:
On the following page are several variations for the BASIC WHOLE WHEAT MUFFIN MIX. Use the MUFFIN MIX just as it reads along with any of these additions. When the instruction reads to leave out certain items this pertains to the original recipe. These variations can also be made into biscuits or baked in mini loaf pans.

SOY, RICE, MILLET OR BUCKWHEAT MUFFINS
Add: 1/2 cup soy, rice, millet or buckwheat flour
Leave out: 1/2 cup whole wheat flour

BARLEY OR OAT MUFFINS
Add: 1 cup barley or oat flour
Leave out: 1 cup whole wheat flour

CORNBREAD or MUFFINS
Add: 1 1/2 cups cornmeal, 3/4 cup white flour and 1 tablespoon oil
Leave out: 1/2 cup of the water and 2 1/2 cups of the whole wheat flour

CAROB MUFFINS
Add: 1/3 cup carob powder, 1/2 cup honey, 1/2 cup chopped nuts,
2 teaspoons vanilla
Leave out: 1/3 cup water

RAISIN ORANGE MUFFINS
Add: 3/4 cup raisins and 1 tablespoon dried orange peel

DATE BRAN MUFFINS
Add: 1/2 cup oat or wheat bran and 1 cup chopped dates
Leave out: 3/4 cup whole wheat flour

CARAWAY RYE MUFFINS
Add: 1 cup rye flour, 2 tablespoons molasses and 1 1/2 teaspoons caraway seed
Leave out: 1 cup whole wheat flour and the honey

BLUEBERRY MUFFINS
Add: 1 1/2 cups fresh blueberries, 1/4 cup honey and 1 teaspoon vanilla
Leave out: 1/2 cup water

PINEAPPLE MUFFINS
Add: 1 can 20 oz. crushed pineapple, well drained, 3 tablespoons honey
and 1 teaspoon vanilla
Leave out: 3/4 cup water

JAM MUFFINS
Add: 3/4 cup DRIED FRUIT JAM
After filling muffin tins drop 3/4-1 teaspoon jam on top of batter then let
rise 10 minutes.

BANANA NUT MUFFINS
Add: 1 3/4 cups mashed bananas, 1/2 cup chopped nuts, 3 tablespoons honey
Leave out: 1 cup water and oil

CHEESE MUFFINS
Add: 2 cups BASIC CHEESE SAUCE
Leave out: 2/3 cup water, 1/2 teaspoon salt and the oil

TAHINI MUFFINS
Add: 1/4 cup tahini
Leave out: oil

CRANBERRY, CARROT, ZUCCHINI OR APPLE MUFFINS
Add: 1/2 cup honey, 1/2 cup chopped nuts, 1 teaspoon coriander (optional), 1 cup packed, grated carrot, zucchini, cranberry or apple

Leave out: 3/4 cup water for each except the cranberry. Leave out 1/2 cup water for the cranberry.

BREAKFASTS

COOKING CHART FOR
WHOLE GRAIN CEREALS

GRAIN (in 1 cup amounts)	WATER	TIME
1. Any rolled or flaked cereal such as rolled oats, barley, rye, wheat	2 1/2 cups	1-1 1/2 hours
2. Quick oats	2 1/2 cups	30 minutes
3. Cornmeal	2 1/2 cups	1 1/2 hours
4. Hulled cereal such as millet, rice, barley, grits, steel cut oats	3 cups	2-3 hours
5. Whole berries such as wheat berries and rye berries	3 cups	3-4 hours

Studies show that when cereals are well cooked so as to break down all of the raw starch grains digestion is easier and, all in all, the benefits gained in health out way the hassle of taking more time to cook.

Stove Top Cooking Directions- Bring water and salt to a boil in a covered saucepan. Stir in grain, cover and return to a boil. Turn heat down to a light boil and cook for recommended length of time. Do not stir grain after mixing with boiling water, as this may cause the cereal to burn in the bottom of the pan. If cereal tends to be stuck in the bottom of the pan at the end of the cooking, simply remove pan from the burner. Leave the lid on and let it sit for 10-15 minutes, then stir. It should come off the bottom easily at this time. Cornmeal will lump when added to boiling water unless part of the water is left cold to stir with the cornmeal before adding to boiling water.

Crock Pot- All cereals, except flaked cereals, do well in a crock pot overnight. Flakes get mushy. Try mixing 2 or 3 for variety in texture and a unique taste. The temperature setting varies with different pots. The cereals needs to come to a simmer or light boil. Usually this is accomplished on a low setting of temperature but sometimes it takes a high setting.

Baking- Any of the cereals may be baked. This is a very easy way to prepare the cereals. This is also a quicker method when baked at 350 degrees. The higher temperature of baking will increase the cooking speed as water boils at 212 degrees and therefore takes longer to thoroughly cook. Use the same amount of water as in the chart, place in a baking dish with the cereal and salt then cover. Begin with hot water to help bring the grain to a boil in the dish sooner. Reduce the time from the cooking chart by 1/3 to 1/2 the cooking time.

Simmer Ring- This is a device to put on the burner. It acts as a heat deflector. It is usually about 1/4-1/2 inch in height and circular to cover the burner. This is the easiest way to avoid burning food on the stove. Just make sure the cereal comes to a light boil. This may mean having the heat a little higher. The deflector usually costs a few dollars and is worth every penny!

Salt- For each cup of water use 1/4 teaspoon of salt or less.

Ways to Shorten Cooking Time:
1. Soaking grains overnight will save about 10 minutes for each hour of cooking.
2. DEXTRINIZING or toasting grains before adding them to water helps to break down raw starch grains. This cuts the cooking time approximately in half. Large quantities of grains may be dextrinized ahead of time and stored the same as those not yet toasted.
See CHART FOR DEXTRINIZING WHOLE GRAIN CEREALS.

CHART FOR DEXTRINIZING WHOLE GRAIN CEREALS

Dextrinizing may be done in the oven or on top of the stove. No water is involved, only dry heat. Grains should take on a light golden brown. When doing grains on top of the stove use a large, flat bottom pan such as a cast iron or stainless steel frying pan. Grains will need constant stirring on medium low heat. For easy stirring do not fill the pan more than half full. For the oven method use a cookie sheet. Grains will need to be stirred 2-3 times during baking. Bake at 250 degrees. See the chart to determine how long the dextrinizing should take. The chart also shows the shortened cooking time once the grain is added to boiling water.

GRAIN	DEXTRINIZING METHOD:		LIGHTLY BOIL IN COVERED PAN:
	OVEN at 250	STOVETOP on medium/low	
Rolled or Flaked	45 minutes	8-10 minutes	20 minutes
Meal	45 minutes	8-10 minutes	30 minutes
Hulled	45 minutes	10-15 minutes	60 minutes

CORN MILLET PORRIDGE

1/2 cup millet
1/2 cup cornmeal
3 1/2 cups boiling water
1/2 cup cool water

1 teaspoon salt
1/2 cup coconut
1 cup chopped dates

Mix cornmeal into cool water then add, with millet and salt, to boiling water. Stir for a few minutes as cornmeal thickens. Cover and let lightly boil for 2 hours. Remove from heat. Stir in coconut and dates. Let sit covered, 15 minutes. Stir again and serve.

NOTE: 1- Cornmeal tends to stick to bottom of the pan during the cooking. Do not stir as this will make it worse. 2- A simmer ring keeps grain from sticking. 3- a crock pot works great with this recipe. Add coconut and dates several minutes before serving. This will make them soft. 4- Use leftover cereal to make a BASIC CEREAL WAFFLE.

FRUITED HOT CEREAL

3 cups hot cooked cereal
1/3 cup NUTS OR SEEDS pg 6

2 cups canned or frozen fruit
1/2 cup chopped dried fruit

Drain and warm fruit. Chop nuts. Stir together all ingredients. Pour into serving dish. May sprinkle with coconut or more chopped nuts. Serve immediately or reheat in oven.

WHOLE BERRY CROCK CEREAL

1 cup whole grain berries
4 1/2 cups hot tap water

1/2 cup millet or rice
1 1/4 teaspoons salt

Combine all in the crock pot and lightly boil overnight. Some crock pots can accomplish this on Low or Medium setting but there are some that must be on High to cook the grain so that the shell bursts.

VARIATION:
After cereal is done cooking, turn off heat. Serve as is or stir in chopped nuts and dried fruit. Cover and let sit 10 minutes. Stir again and serve.

GLORIFIED RICE

3 cups cooked rice
1 1/2 cups pineapple juice
1 20 oz. can crushed pineapple
1 cup chopped dried fruit

1/2-1 cup chopped nuts
1/4 teaspoon salt
2 teaspoons vanilla
1/2 cup additional cooked cereal

Blend 3/4 cup of the juice with additional cereal (may be rice or any other kind) and 1/4 cup of the nuts or seeds. Stir all ingredients together and let sit a few hours before serving for flavors to blend. May serve hot or cold.

BAKED OATS

2 1/2 cups hot water or juice
1/2 teaspoon salt

1 2/3 cups quick or rolled oats

Dissolve salt into water or juice. Mix together with oats in a 1 quart casserole. Bake at 350 degrees, covered, 45 minutes.

OAT FRUIT BAKE

3 cups quick or rolled oats
1 cup chopped dried fruit
2 chopped apples

3 3/4 cups hot water or apple juice
1/2 cup chopped nuts
1 1/4 teaspoons salt

Mix all together in a 2 quart casserole. Bake at 350, covered, 45 minutes.

LEFTOVER CEREAL DELIGHT

2 cups leftover cooked cereal
2 cups bread or waffle crumbs
1/4 cup coconut

1/2 cup chopped dried fruit
2 cups soy or nut milk

Stir together all except coconut. Pour into 2 quart casserole and let sit. Top with coconut. Serve hot or cold.

SIMPLE GRANOLA

1 2/3 cups water
1/3 cup oil
1/4 cup SWEETENER pg 6
1 tablespoon vanilla
2 teaspoons salt

12 cups quick or rolled oats
1 cup chopped dried fruit
1 cup chopped nuts or sunflower
  seeds

Stir together well first five ingredients. Add oats and nuts, stirring only enough to moisten oats. Spread out on two cookie sheets. Bake at 200 for 2-2 1/2 hours, until dry, stirring every 30-40 minutes. Add fruit after baking.

PEANUT BUTTER GRANOLA

6 cups quick or rolled oats
1 cup whole grain flour
1/2 cup water

1/3 cup honey
1/2 cup peanut butter
1 teaspoon salt

Stir together well all but oats and flour. Add oats and flour stirring only enough to moisten the dry ingredients. Spread out on one cookie sheet. Bake at 200 for 2-2 1/2 hours, until dry. Stir 2 or 3 times while baking.

BANANA NUT GRANOLA

1 1/4 cups dates
1/2 cup water
2 bananas
1 tablespoon vanilla

1 1/2 teaspoons salt
10 cups rolled oats
2 cups chopped nuts or sunflower seeds

Bring water and dates to a boil in a covered saucepan. Remove from heat. Let sit 5 minutes then blend smooth with all but the last 2 ingredients. Stir all ingredients together. Spread on two cookie sheets. Bake at 200 degrees for 2-2 1/2 hours, stirring 2-3 times while baking.

MUESLI

2 1/4 cups granola of choice
2 cups chopped apples
2 cups apple juice or juice of choice

1/4 cup chopped dried fruit or raisins
1/4 cup chopped nuts or raw sunflower seeds

Combine all ingredients. Refrigerator several hours before serving.

SWISS STYLE GRANOLA

2 cups applesauce

2 cups granola of choice

Mix sauce and granola. Let sit a few hours. Serve hot or cold. Serve plain or with nondairy milk.

HOT GRANOLA

1 cup granola or Grape Nuts   2 1/2 cups fruit juice, soy milk

Lightly boil all ingredients in a covered saucepan, 5-10 minutes.

COBBLER

10 cups sliced or chopped fruit   1 cup juice or water
1 1/2 tablespoons cornstarch   2 tablespoons SWEETENER,
1 cup chopped dried fruit   optional pg 6
                                                          1 recipe DROP BISCUITS

Fruit may be fresh, frozen or canned and should be drained. If fruit is small, such as, blueberries then use whole. Dissolve cornstarch and sweetener in juice then mix with fruit. Pour into a 9 1/2x13 1/2 baking dish. Mix up the biscuits and drop by tablespoons on top of the fruit with batter about 1/4-1/2 inches apart. Let raise 10 minutes. Bake at 350 degrees for 35-40 minutes or until bread is golden brown.

CRISP

TOPPING:
3 tablespoons SWEETENER pg 6   1 1/2 teaspoons coriander, opt.
3 tablespoons oil   1 teaspoon vanilla
1/3 cup water   1/2 cup whole grain flour
1/2 teaspoon salt   3 cups quick or rolled oats

Combine wet and dry ingredients separately. Mix together.

FRUIT MIXTURE:
7 cups sliced or chopped fruit   1 tablespoon cornstarch
3/4 cup juice or water   2 tablespoons SWEETENER pg 6
1/2 cup chopped dried fruit

Dissolve starch and sweetener into juice. Add this with the fruit to an 8x11 casserole. Top with oat topping. Bake at 350 degrees for 40 minutes or until golden brown. Serve plain, with nondairy milk, fruit sauce or BANANA ICE CREAM. Hot or cold. For the fruit mixture try a mixture of fruits.

VARIATION:
For another oat topping try 4 cups unbaked granola from recipes in this book.

BREAD PUDDING

3 cups cubed bread   1/2 cup DRIED FRUIT JAM
3 cups shredded or chopped apples   2 tablespoons peanut butter

Stir together jam and peanut butter. Combine all ingredients and place in a 1 1/2 quart, covered casserole. Bake at 350 degrees for 35 minutes. Serve plain or with nondairy milk.

SALTY OIL-FREE POPCORN

2 1/2 tablespoons salt   1 cup water

Use method of choice to pop popcorn without oil. Then spray with salt water. One of the following methods may be used to help dry the popcorn after being sprayed or serve as is.

1. OVEN METHOD: After corn is popped spray corn several times (10-15 times for 1/2 c. unpopped popcorn).Put popped corn on a cookie sheet and heat in a hot oven after it has been sprayed with salt water. Heat for a few minutes. Watch for burning.

2. MICROWAVE METHOD: After corn is popped spray corn several times (10-15 times for 1/2 c. unpopped popcorn). Heat in microwave for 10 seconds then stir. Heat again for 10 seconds and stir. This should make the popcorn fairly dry. Over heating will toughen popcorn.

DIXIE TOAST

2 large bananas   1/2 cup cashews
1 1/2 cups water   1 teaspoon vanilla
1/2 teaspoon salt

Blend smooth all ingredients. Pour into bowl. Dip slices of bread into batter. This will cover about 16 slices of bread. Choose one of the following methods to finish the toast. See WAFFLE TIPS-WAYS TO SERVE pg 24.

METHOD #1 Frying - Brown on a non-stick skillet on medium heat.
METHOD #2 Broiling - Place on oiled cookie sheet and brown on each side.
METHOD #3 Baking - Place on oiled cookie sheet. Bake at 350 degrees 20-30 minutes or when golden brown on bottom. Flip and bake an additional 10-15 minutes.

FRENCH TOAST

1 cup quick or rolled oats
1/3 cup cashews
1 3/4 cups water

1 teaspoon salt
2 tablespoons SWEETENER pg 6

Blend smooth all ingredients. Follow spreading directions and choose one of the cooking methods outlined under DIXIE TOAST. For suggested toppings see WAFFLE TIPS - WAYS TO SERVE on page 24.

APPLE ICING BREAD

1 recipe for BASIC WHOLE WHEAT BREAD (use only 1 teaspoon yeast)
3 cups apple sauce
1/2 cup chopped dried fruit

1/2 cup chopped nuts
1/4 cup coconut

Roll out dough 1/4 inch thick onto an oiled cookie sheet. Let raise 10 minutes. Cover with fruit sauce then evenly sprinkle remaining items on top. Bake at 350 degrees for 35-40 minutes.

VARIATIONS:
1. Leave out nuts and spread a thin layer of EMULSIFIED PEANUT BUTTER or HOMEMADE NUT BUTTER on the dough before the fruit sauce.
2. Slice 2 bananas on the dough before the fruit sauce.

PANCAKES

1 1/2 cups water
1 cup quick or rolled oats
1 cup tofu

2 tablespoons NUTS OR SEEDS
1/2 teaspoon salt
1 teaspoon SWEETENER pg 6

Blend smooth all ingredients. Let sit 5 minutes. Preheat nonstick skillet on medium heat. Pour batter into pan in 1/4 cup portions. Slightly flatten with bottom of measuring cup. Flip when bottom is golden, 5-10 minutes. Cook the same on other side. See WAFFLE TIPS-WAYS TO SERVE on page 24 for suggestions on toppings.

VARIATION:
Substitute 1/2 cup SOYBASE, page 63, for the tofu.

WAFFLE TIPS

1. CONDITIONING WAFFLE IRON - Irons with non-stick surfaces should always be oiled after being washed. Use a food release spray such as Pam. Repeat oiling when waffles begin to stick to grids. Over baking waffles and over heating the iron before pouring on the batter will make it necessary to oil the waffle iron more often. Overheating is happening when the oil is smoking. Iron is ready for batter when water drops spatter on hot grid. Several waffles can be made on a nonstick iron without spraying with oil in between waffles when following the above guidelines.

2. Large quantities of soybeans may be soaked ahead, drained and frozen for SOY OAT WAFFLES.

3. BAKING TIME - 6-inch irons bake in 8-10 minutes. 9-inch irons take 15-20 minutes. Longer baking (20 minutes) is preferred to help insure breakdown of raw starches for good digestion.

4. STORAGE - Stack cooled waffles in a plastic bag and freeze or store for a few days in the refrigerator.

5. REHEATING - (A) For crisp waffles: (1) in the toaster; (2) directly on oven racks for 5-10 minutes at 350 degrees.
(B) For soft waffles: (1) Place in a covered casserole for 15-20 minutes at 350 degrees (2) Cover and place in microwave on high until warm.

6. WAYS TO SERVE - Top with (1) CAROB MILLET SAUCE (2) MILLET PUDDING (3) ICE CREAM (4) FRUIT SOUP (5) FRUIT SAUCE (6) FRUIT TOPPING (7) applesauce or other fruit sauce (8) canned or frozen fruit, drained. Add fruit to thicken juice or juice concentrate (1 cup juice and 2 tablespoons cornstarch).
In place of butter use: (1) HOMEMADE NUT BUTTER (2) EMULSIFIED PEANUT BUTTER (3) MILLET BUTTER (4) peanut butter or other nut butters.

7. Other uses for waffles - (1) bread for yeast-free or wheat-free or gluten-free diets, (2) bread crumbs, (3) WAFFLE CAKE.

OAT WAFFLE

2 cups quick or rolled oats   **1/2 teaspoon salt**
2 cups water

Blend smooth all ingredients. Pour into hot waffle iron. Bake 15-20 minutes. See WAFFLE TIPS for how to condition iron and ways to serve. Makes 1 1/2-9 inch waffles.

VARIATION:
Substitute 1/2 cup of the oats for another rolled cereal or cornmeal.

SOY OAT WAFFLE

1 cup soaked soybeans   **2 1/4 cups water**
1 1/2 cups quick or rolled oats   **3/4 teaspoon salt**

Soak 1 cup of raw soybeans in 3 cups of water for about 8 hours. Drain off water. This will make 2 1/2 cups of soaked beans. Blend smooth all ingredients. Pour into a hot waffle iron. Bake 20 minutes. See WAFFLE TIPS for how to condition iron and ways to serve. Makes 2-9 inch waffles.

VARIATIONS:
1. Substitute soaked, raw garbanzos for soybeans.
2. Substitute 1/2 cup of the oats for another rolled cereal or corn meal.
3. Substitute soy or nut milk for the water.

NUT OAT WAFFLE

2 cups quick or rolled oats   **3/4 teaspoon salt**
2 1/2 cups water   **1 teaspoon vanilla or maple ext.**
3 tablespoons pecans   **2 teaspoons SWEETENER pg 6**

Blend smooth all ingredients. Pour into hot waffle iron. Bake 15-20 minutes. See WAFFLE TIPS for how to condition iron and ways to serve. Makes 2-9 inch waffles.

VARIATIONS:
1. Substitute soy milk for water.
2. Substitute any other NUTS OR SEEDS, page 6, for pecans.

CEREAL WAFFLE

3-4 cups of leftover cooked cereal (millet, rice, oatmeal, barley...)

Spread cereal with a spoon into a hot waffle iron. (If cooking cereal to make waffles try reducing salt by 1/4 of normal use.) Bake 15-20 minutes. See WAFFLE TIPS for how to condition iron. Makes 2-9 inch waffles.

CHEESE AND MILK SUBSTITUTES

SOY MILK

1/2 cup SOYBASE pg 63 or tofu
1/3 cup cashews
1/2 cup water
1 teaspoon vanilla

2 tablespoons SWEETENER pg 6
1/4 teaspoon salt
3 1/2 cups additional water

Blend smooth all but additional water. When smooth add remaining water. Chill. Stir before pouring.

VARIATIONS:
1. Add 2 cups of fresh, canned or frozen fruit to the recipe, such as bananas, peaches or strawberries. Choose 1 or 2 fruits.
2. Add 1 cup of dried fruit. This should first be soften 5 minutes in 1 cup of hot water. Use water from the recipe.
3. Replace cashews with 1/4 cup oil or other NUTS OR SEEDS, page 6.

CAROB MILK:
Add 1/4 cup carob powder and 1 tablespoon of additional sweetener.

NUT MILK

1 cup raw cashews
1 cup hot water
3 tablespoons SWEETENER pg 6

1 teaspoon vanilla
3/4 teaspoon salt
5 cups additional cold water

Blend smooth all but additional water. When smooth add remaining water.

LEMON COCONUT MILK

1/2 cup coconut
1/2 cup leftover cooked cereal
1 1/2 cups pineapple juice
1/2 teaspoon salt

1/2 teaspoon lemon extract
1 cup water
1/2 cup additional cold water

Blend smooth all but juice and additional water then add when smooth.

CREAMY MILK

2/3 cup cooked cereal

1 teaspoon vanilla

1/3 cup cashews
1/2 cup dates
1 cup boiling water

1/8 teaspoon salt
2 cups addition water

Pour boiling water over dates. Let stand 5 minutes. Blend smooth all except additional water. Add remaining water when ingredients are smooth.

GOLDEN SAUCE

3/4 cup cooked potatoes
1/2 cup cooked carrots
1 1/4 cups water

1 teaspoon salt
2 tablespoons YEAST FLAKES
2 tablespoons cashews

Blend smooth all ingredients. Heat and serve over vegetables, rice, pasta.

VARIATIONS: Substitute cashews with 2 tablespoons TOASTED sesame seeds or 1 teaspoon toasted sesame seed oil.

TENDER LOW-CAL CHEESE

2 cups water
1/3 cup pimento
1/3 cup white flour
1/4 cup YEAST FLAKES pg 6

1 1/2 tablespoons lemon juice
1/2 cup cashews
2 teaspoons onion powder
2 teaspoons salt

Blend smooth all but 1 cup of water. Empty into sauce pan. Rinse blender with remaining water. Add to pan. Lightly boil 5-10 minutes, stirring. Serve warm over vegetables, beans, potatoes or HAY STACKS. Chill for spread.

VARIATION: May substitute 3 tablespoons oil for nuts. This variation works well for MACARONI AND CHEESE.

CHEESE SPREAD

1/4 cup quick or rolled oats
1/4 cup NUTS OR SEEDS pg 6
1 cup water
2 tablespoons tomato paste
3 tablespoons YEAST FLAKES pg 6

1 teaspoon salt
1 teaspoon onion powder
1/2 teaspoon garlic powder
1 tablespoon lemon juice

Place all ingredients in blender. Blend smooth. Lightly boil in sauce pan, stirring about 5 minutes, until thickened. Use on bread, crackers, vegetables or as a vegetable dip.

BASIC CHEESE SAUCE

1 cup water	1/3 cup pimento
1 cup cashews	1 teaspoon salt
2 tablespoon YEAST FLAKES pg 6	1 teaspoon onion powder
1 1/2 tablespoons lemon juice	1/4 teaspoon garlic powder

Blend smooth all ingredients. Chilling will make sauce thicker. Use over salads, cooked vegetables, pasta, rice, potatoes, or on pizza or lasagna.

VARIATIONS:
1. Substitute other NUTS or SEEDS, page 6, for half or all of the cashews. Try almonds with the brown skins removed (blanched, page 6) as brown flecks show up in cheese or try raw sunflower seeds.

2. To give an orange color without the pimento substitute 2/3 cup cooked carrots. A little more water may be necessary to blend. OR pimento may be left out or reduced, it is only for color.

3. COOKED CHEESE: Leave out 1/2 cup of cashews. After blending cheese pour into a sauce pan and bring to a light boil for about 3 minutes, stirring. Cooked cashews thicken when cooled. Cooking enhances the flavor of the cheese.

4. SLICING CHEESE: Leave out 1/2 cup cashews. Add 3 tablespoons Emes Plain Kosher Jel. Bring to a boil the water from the original recipe. Blend smooth all ingredients with the boiling water. Chill several hours then slice cheese or cut in cubes. Melts when exposed to heat. Freezes well.

5. ECONOMY CHEESE: Substitute 1/2 cup hot cooked pasta, millet or rice for 1/2 cup of the cashews.

6. BEAN CASHEW CHEESE: Substitute 1 cup drained cooked beans for 1/2 cup of the cashews. Using a light colored bean such as garbanzos, soys, navy beans will keep the cheese the original color. A darker bean can be used but will effect the color.

7. TOFU CHEESE: Substitute 3/4 cup of Mori-Nu Firm or Extra Firm Tofu for 1/2 cup cashews. Leave out 1/4 cup of the water from the original recipe.

8. CARAWAY CHEESE: Add 1 teaspoon of caraway seed while blending. Leave out the pimento.

9. GARLIC HERB CHEESE: Leave out the pimento. Add 1-2 cloves of garlic, 1/4 teaspoon basil, 1/4 teaspoon dill weed while blending. Stir in 1 teaspoon dry parsley flakes after blending.

10. SMOKED CHEESE: Add 1/4 teaspoon of liquid hickory smoke flavor.

11. TOASTED SESAME CHEESE: Substitute 1/4 cup TOASTED sesame seeds, page 63, for 1/4 cup cashews. Blend longer as sesame seeds do not blend smooth as easily as cashews. OR add 1-2 teaspoons of toasted sesame seed oil while blending. This toasted oil may be purchased at a health food store.

12. DILLY CHEESE: Add 1/2 teaspoon dill weed while blending.

13. SPICY CHEESE: Add 2 teaspoons cumin while blending.

14. PESTO CHEESE: Add 1 teaspoon of PESTO recipe, page 46.

15. DRIED PIMENTO CHEESE: Use dried pimento in place of canned pimento. This can be a money saver if buying pimento in large cans and drying it in a food dryer. OR buy dried sweet red pepper flakes in bulk OR get sweet red peppers by the bushel in season from a produce market, or grow your own then chop up and dry. No blanching is needed. 3 cups canned pimento at a weight of 28 ounces equal 1 3/4 cups dried flakes at a weight of 1 1/2 ounces! Flakes may be blended in the blender to make a powder at this time if desired. This really saves on storage space. Add 3 tablespoons of the pimento flakes or 2 teaspoons ground pimento powder while blending sauce.

16. See FOOD DRYING-CHEESE page 70. Easy, many uses, creative.

17. FREEZING DIRECTIONS: Any of these variations may be frozen except the TOFU CHEESE. The SLICING CHEESE will retain its original shape when thawed. The remaining cheese variations will need to be reheated to return to original shape. When cheese is frozen then thawed it has a chunky, watery look. To reheat put the thawed sauce in a sauce pan. Lightly boil, stirring, for about 3 minutes, until smooth again. Use immediately or chill to make cheese thicker.

NOTE:
Variations 8-15 may be used with the Basic Cheese Sauce or any of the variations 1-7. For example, prepare variation #4, Slicing Cheese, and use flavoring of variation #7, Caraway Cheese. End product is a caraway cheese that can be sliced. Or use #5, Economy Cheese combined with #12, Dilly Cheese. You have the potential of making 64 different cheese recipes!!!

AGAR CHEESE

1 cup water	1 tablespoon lemon juice
2 tablespoons Agar Flakes	2 tablespoons YEAST FLAKES
1/3 cup cashews	1 teaspoon salt
1/2 cup water	1/2 teaspoon onion powder
3 tablespoons pimento, optional	1/8 teaspoon garlic powder

Agar Flakes are dried sea weed used for thickening. They can be purchased where health foods are sold. Lightly boil first 2 ingredients for 3 to 5 minutes, until flakes are clear, stirring. Blend smooth remaining ingredients.Then empty sauce pan into blender by scraping with a rubber spatula to insure getting all the agar off the sides of the pan. Blend again. Pour into container and chill. This cheese can be sliced. When warmed it gives a slight melting effect. Good for GRILLED CHEESE or sandwiches. Cheese does not freeze well.

SHREDDED AGAR CHEESE:

Add one additional tablespoon of Agar Flakes to the original recipe. This cheese can be nicely shred on a manual, hand held shredder. Use shredded cheese on dishes such as pizza, lasagna, salads or where shredded cheese is used and looks attractive. The cheese will not melt.

Dry this cheese in a food dryer. See Food Drying section, page 71. It works very well this way.

SHREDDED TOFU CHEESE

1 box, 12.3 oz., firm or extra firm Mori-Nu tofu

1/2 teaspoon salt	1/2 teaspoon onion powder
1/4 teaspoon garlic powder	2 tablespoons YEAST FLAKES

Shred tofu by hand on a manual, hand held shredder, a food processor will mash the tofu. Gently stir in seasonings. Spray a non-stick skillet with a food release spray or lightly oil. Spread ingredients out on the skillet to make a thin layer. Cook on medium heat. Gently turn with a spatula occasionally. Fry about 15 minutes. As it cooks it looses some of the water in the tofu and becomes tender yet firm and will not crumble easily. Use shredded cheese on dishes such as pizza, lasagna, salads or where shredded cheese is used and looks attractive. The cheese will not melt nor can it be dried as the cheese above. This cheese does not freeze well.

DESSERTS

ORCHARD APPLE PIE

2 cups shredded raw apple   **1/3 cup granulated tapioca**
2 cups pineapple juice

Lightly boil juice and tapioca, stirring. Cook until tapioca is clear. Cool slightly then add apples. Chill. Pour into baked pie crust. May sprinkle TOASTED coconut on top or serve with TOFU WHIPPED CREAM or CREAMY LOW-CAL TOPPING.

VARIATIONS:
1. Stir in 1/4 cup chopped dried fruit and 1/4 cup NUTS or SEEDS, page 6.
2. Substitute 1 cup of juice concentrate of choice with 1 cup of water for pineapple juice.
3. Pie may be used as a main dish if using an oil free crust such as the OAT FRUIT PIE CRUST.

LEMON PINEAPPLE PIE

1/2 cup cashews   **1/4 teaspoon lemon extract**
1/2 cup water   **1/4 teaspoon salt**
3 tablespoons lemon juice   **1/3 cup cornstarch**
2 tablespoons SWEETENER pg 6   **2 1/2 cups pineapple juice**
1 teaspoon vanilla   **3/4 cup crushed pineapple**

Blend smooth, first eight ingredients. Pour into sauce pan. Rinse blender with juice then add to sauce pan. Lightly boil 5-10 minutes, stirring, until thickened. Stir in well drained crushed pineapple. Pour into baked pie shell and chill or serve in custard dishes. Sprinkle TOASTED coconut on top or serve with TOFU WHIPPED CREAM or CREAMY LOW-CAL TOPPING.

BERRY PIE

4 cups fresh berries   **1/4 cup water**
1/3 cup cornstarch   **1/8 teaspoon salt**
1 1/4 cups unsweetened juice concentrate of choice

Lightly boil, stirring about 5-10 minutes until thickened, all but fruit. Remove from heat and stir in fruit. If using large berries, such as strawberries, they should be sliced first. Pour into baked pie shell. Chill. May sprinkle

TOASTED coconut on top or serve with TOFU WHIPPED CREAM or CREAMY LOW-CAL TOPPING.

VARIATION:
Substitute chopped grapes mixed with unsweetened white grape juice concentrate. Grapes may be chopped by hand or chopped briefly in a food processor. Drain off juice if using a food processor. Measure the grapes as 4 cups after chopping and draining.

MILLET PUDDING

1 cup pineapple juice	**2 tablespoons cashews**
1 cup hot, cooked millet	**1/8 teaspoon salt**
1 teaspoon vanilla	

Blend smooth all ingredients. Chill to thicken.

Ways to serve:
1. Sprinkle 1/4 inch of granola or Grape Nuts in bottom of a flat dish. Spoon pudding over, 1 inch thick. Chill. Add a thickened fruit topping of choice before serving or try FRUIT TOPPING, page 36.
2. Stir in 1/2-1 cup fruit, i.e., drained pineapple chunks, banana slices, berries, then chill. Serve as is or over WAFFLES, FRENCH TOAST, PAN-CAKES or cereal.
3. Layer in a parfait glass with granola, pudding and sliced fruit (fruit may be canned or frozen and drained or use fresh fruit). Try STRAWBERRY JAM or FRUIT TOPPING in place of fruit. Repeat layers until glass is full.

MILLET PINEAPPLE PUDDING:
Bring juice to a boil with 1/3 cup chopped dried pineapple pieces. Let fruit soften 5 minutes then blend all ingredients together until smooth. Use a little additional juice to blend if needed.

MILLET TOFU PUDDING:
Bring juice to a boil with 2/3 cup chopped dried pineapple pieces. Let fruit soften 5 minutes. Blend all ingredients smooth using a few tablespoons of additional juice as needed to properly blend ingredients. Empty blender and blend smooth 1 package of 12.3 oz. Firm or Extra Firm Mori-Nu Tofu. Use 1 or 2 tablespoons of juice to blend the tofu smooth if necessary. Combine all and chill. Tofu gives lightness to pudding.

VARIATION:
Substitute dried papaya pieces for pineapple for a pretty salmon color.

CAROB PUDDING

4 cups soy or nut milk
1/3 cup SWEETENER pg 6
1/4 cup carob powder
1/3 cup cornstarch

1/2 teaspoon salt
1 teaspoon vanilla
1 1/2 teaspoon coffee subst. opt.
    such as Roma, Cafix or Pero

Stir or blend all ingredients until smooth. Pour into a sauce pan. Lightly boil, stirring until thickened, about 5 minutes. Pour into serving dish or individual bowls, chill. Serve as is or sprinkle TOASTED coconut on top or serve with TOFU WHIPPED CREAM or CREAMY LOW-CAL TOPPING.

CAROB PIE:
To serve as a pie use 1/2 cup cornstarch.

OIL-FREE PIE CRUST

Try the cracker recipe for BREAD STICKS or the OAT FRUIT PIE CRUST.

OAT FRUIT PIE CRUST

1 1/4 cups quick oats
1/2 cup applesauce

1/4 teaspoon salt

Mix and mold into an oiled pie dish. Bake at 350 degrees, 20-25 minutes.

WHOLE WHEAT PIE CRUST

1/2 cup oat flour
1/2 cup whole wheat flour
1/4 teaspoon salt

2 tablespoons oil
1/4 cup water

Blend quick or rolled oats fine to make flour. Mix dry and wet ingredients separately. Combine together, stirring with a fork. Stir as little as possible. Then, either press dough into an oiled pie pan by hand or roll out dough between two layers of plastic wrap, then lay in pan. Poke in a few places with a fork. Bake at 350 degrees for 13-15 minutes.

FRUIT NUT CAKE

1/2 cup warm water
2 tablespoons yeast

3/4 cup chopped dried fruit
1 teaspoon vanilla

1 tablespoon SWEETENER pg 6	1 1/2 teaspoons salt
1/2 cup honey	2 cups whole wheat flour
1/2 cup chopped NUTS OR SEEDS	1 cup white flour
1 1/3 cups mashed bananas (3 med. size)	

Mix together water, sweetener and yeast. Let sit 5 minutes. Add to this all but 2 cups of flour. Stir in flour. Beat batter 1-2 minute. Place in an oiled 8x8 inch cake pan or two 3x7 inch loaf pans. Let rise 15 minutes. Bake at 350 degrees for 45 minutes. Remove from pan. Serve as is or frost.

WAFFLE CAKE

This recipe is based on 4-9 inch waffles. Adjust according to the size of your waffles. May prefer to use 3 waffles. Use one of the following fillings.

1 1/2 recipes of chilled CAROB PUDDING plus banana slices.
1 1/2 recipes of warm BERRY PIE filling.
2 recipes of warm ORCHARD APPLE PIE filling.
2 recipes of chilled LEMON PINEAPPLE PIE filling plus addtional crushed pineapple, sliced grapes, strawberries or peaches.
3 recipes of chilled MILLET PUDDING plus sliced fruit.
3 recipes of chilled CAROB MILLET SAUCE plus sliced fruit.

Frost each waffle with about 1 cup filling. Stack one on top of another like a layer cake. Additional fruit may be layered on top of filling on each waffle. On top waffle put remaining filling allowing it to drizzle over sides. Insert toothpicks on top then cover with plastic wrap. Chill at least 3-4 hours. Serve as is or with TOFU WHIPPED CREAM or CREAMY LOW-CAL TOPPING. Serve as a main dish or as a dessert.

FUDGY CAROB BROWNIES

3/4 cup honey	1/3 cup oil
2 cups whole wheat flour	1/2 cup carob powder
2/3 cup chopped walnuts	1 teaspoon salt
2/3 cup water	1 teaspoon vanilla
1 1/2 teaspoons coffee substitute, opt. such as Roma, Cafix or Pero	

Stir until smooth all but flour, then add flour. Bake at 350 degrees for 35 minutes in an oiled 8x8 inch pan. Remove from pan to cool. Frost.

TOFU CHEESE CAKE

2 packages 12.3 oz. Firm or Extra Firm Mori-Nu Tofu
2 teaspoons vanilla   **1 cup water**
1/4 teaspoon almond or lemon extract **1/4 cup cashews**
1/2 teaspoon salt   **1/2 cup rice syrup, sugar**
3 tablespoons Emes Plain Kosher Jel   **or honey**

Blend smooth 1 box of tofu with extracts and salt then empty. Heat water until very hot. Add remaining box of tofu, Emes, sweetener, cashews and hot water to blender and blend smooth. Blend on low at first with lid held on securely as hot water tends to create pressure when blended and may push the lid of blender to pop off. Stir ingredients together and spoon over CRUMB CRUST in an 8x8 baking dish. Chill. Serve with FRUIT TOPPING.

NOTE: Rice syrup, cane sugar crystals or sugar may be preferred because they are more mild in flavor than most honey.

VARIATIONS:
THICKENED WITH AGAR FLAKES: Follow instructions above except substitute 3 tablespoons of Agar Flakes for the Emes. The only different step is that the Agar needs to be lightly boil for 3-5 minutes with the water, stirring, until flakes are clear. Use a rubber spatula to empty the sauce pan contents into the blender. This insures getting the flakes that may be stuck to sides of pan. Then blend with remaining tofu, cashews and sweetener.

THICKENED WITH CORNSTARCH: Substitute 1/3 cup starch for the Emes. Leave out 1 box of tofu, use 1/2 cup cashews instead of 1/4 cup. Cut sweetener to 1/3 cup.
First blend tofu, salt and extracts. Next cook the water, sweetener and starch together, stirring, until very thick, then blend with the cashews. Finally stir together all ingredients and spoon on to crust. Making Cheese Cake with cornstarch sets up fine and can be sliced but the consistency of using Emes or Agar Flakes is a little lighter and more firm.

NOTE: Do not do the step with the thickener first with these variations as congealing will begin before the remaining ingredients are ready to add.

CRUMB CRUST

1 cup granola or Grape Nuts

Blend cereal to a fine consistency. Spread in an 8x8 dish. Spoon on filling.

FRUIT TOPPING

1 cup unsweetened fruit juice concentrate
2 tablespoons cornstarch
3 cups finely chopped, mashed or crushed fruit, drained

Lightly boil juice and starch, stirring, until thickened. Fruit can be canned or fresh, try mashing by hand or using a food processor briefly on the fruit. Stir all ingredients together. Chill. If using frozen fruit it should be thawed and drained then mashed to measure 3 cups.

MILLET TOFU CHEESE CAKE

1 package 12.3 oz. Firm or Extra Firm Mori-Nu Tofu
2 tablespoons Emes Plain Kosher Jel
1/4 teaspoon almond or lemon extract

1/2 teaspoon salt	**1/2 cup rice syrup, sugar or honey**
1 cup cooked millet	**1/4 cup cashews**
2 teaspoons vanilla	**1 cup water**

Blend tofu with extracts and salt until smooth then empty into bowl. Heat water and millet until hot. Add to the blender the Emes, sweetener, cashews, hot water and millet and blend until smooth. Blend on low at first with lid held on securely as hot water tends to create pressure when blended and may push the lid to pop off. Stir ingredients together and spoon over CRUMB CRUST in an 8x8 baking dish. Chill. Serve with FRUIT TOPPING.

NOTE: Rice syrup, cane sugar crystals or sugar may be preferred because they are more mild in flavor than most honey.

VARIATIONS:
THICKENED WITH AGAR FLAKES: Blend tofu, salt and extracts. Substitute 2 tablespoons of Agar Flakes for the Emes. The only different step is that the Agar needs to be lightly boil for 3-5 minutes with the water, stirring, until flakes are clear. Add the millet to the pan to get it hot as millet will blend more smoothly when hot. Use a rubber spatula to empty the pan contents into the blender. This insures getting the flakes that may be stuck to sides of pan. Then blend smooth with cashews and sweetener.

THICKENED WITH CORNSTARCH: Substitute 1/3 cup starch for the Emes. Blend tofu, salt and extracts. Next cook the water, sweetener, millet and starch together, stirring, until very thick, then blend with the cashews. Empy blender and stir together all ingredients then spoon onto crust. Chill. Making Cheese Cake with cornstarch sets up fine and can be sliced but the consistency of using Emes or Agar Flakes is a little lighter and more firm.

NOTE: Do not do the step with the thickener first with these variations as congealing will begin before the remaining ingredients are ready to add.

NUTTY CANDY

2/3 cup honey or rice syrup	2 cups Rice Crispies
1 cup coconut	1/4 cup chopped nuts
1/2 cup peanut butter or other nut butter	

Measure out all ingredients first. Lightly boil sweetener 2 minutes, stirring. Quickly combine all items. Roll small balls in hands. Place on plate. Becomes firm in a few hours.Coconut is good when toasted, page 63.

NUTTY CAROB CANDY:

Add 3 tablespoons of carob powder to honey then cook. May also add 3/4 teaspoon peppermint extract just after cooking before adding remaining items.

CREAMY LOW-CAL TOPPING

1 1/4 cups water	1/4 teaspoon salt
1/4 cup SWEETENER pg 6	1 teaspoon vanilla
1/4 cup white flour	1/4 cup cashews

Blend smooth all ingredients except 1/2 cup of the water. Empty into pan. Rinse blender with remaining water then add to pan. Simmer, stirring, until thickened. Chill.

VARIATIONS: Substitiute vanilla for one of the following extracts: 1/4 teaspoon butterscotch, almond, maple OR 1/8 teaspoon lemon.

COCONUT FROSTING

1 cup water	1 tablespoon cornstarch
1/3 cup coconut	1/4 cup SWEETENER pg 6
1/2 cup cashews	1/4 teaspoon salt
1 teaspoon vanilla	

Blend smooth all ingredients. Lightly boil, stirring, until thickened. Chill.

VARIATIONS: (leave out vanilla and add)
1/2 teaspoon lemon, orange, or butterscotch extract OR

1/4 teaspoon maple, anise, cherry or almond extract OR
1 tablespoon carob powder

CAROB PEANUT BUTTER FROSTING

1/2 cup DRIED FRUIT JAM made from dates OR 1/4 cup SWEETENER
1/3 cup peanut butter or other nut butter
3 tablespoons carob powder   **1 tablespoon cornstarch**
1/8 teaspoon   **1 teaspoon vanilla**
1 cup water

Mix together in a sauce pan. Lightly boil, stirring, until thickened. Chill. May also use as spread.

TOFU WHIPPED CREAM

1 package 12.3 oz. Firm or Extra Firm Mori-Nu Tofu
3 tablespoons SWEETENER pg 6   2 tablespoons oil, optional
1/8 teaspoon salt   1 1/2 teaspoons vanilla

Blend smooth all ingredients. Chill.

FRUIT BARS

2 cups quick or rolled oats   1/2 cup SWEETENER pg 6
1 1/2 cups oat flour   1 teaspoon salt
1/2 cup coconut   1/2 cup water
2/3 cup NUTS OR SUNFLOWER SEEDS pg 6

Make oat flour by blending fine 1 1/2 cups oats. Combine dry ingredients. Blend until smooth nuts and water. If using a liquid sweetener such as honey stir it in with blended nuts before adding to dry ingredients. Combine wet and dry ingredients and work the wet throughout so that the ingredients are well mixed. This may work better by using hands instead of a spoon. Put half of the mixture in an oiled 9 1/2 x 13 1/2 baking dish. Gently pat mixture down with the back of a teaspoon that is periodically moistened with water to keep the crumb mixture from sticking to the spoon.

FILLING:
2 recipes of DRIED FRUIT JAM or about 3 cups

Spread filling and top with remaining crumb mixture. Pat down slightly. Bake at 350 degrees for 30-35 minutes. Recipe freezes well.

PEANUT BUTTER CUPS

1 1/2 cups carob chips | 1/2 cup peanut butter or other nut butter

Slowly heat ingredients in a sauce pan. Do not continue to heat once carob has melted as sometimes the consistency begins to change if over-heated. Drop by teaspoons onto a cookie sheet covered with wax paper or plastic wrap. When hardened put in bag or covered dish. May store in freezer or refrigerator. Good frozen. Or fill 1/2 oz. party nut cups and freeze.

VARIATIONS:
1. Add 1 1/2 cups Rice Crispies or Brown Rice Crisps. Empty into baking dish. Flatten to about 1 inch high. Cut into bars when firm. OR drop by teaspoons as mentioned above.
2. 1/3 cup chopped nuts or TOASTED coconut, page 63, may be added.
3. Chunky peanut butter may be used.

CAROB BALLS

1/4 cup carob powder
1/4 cup soy milk powder
1/2 cup honey

1 cup peanut butter or other nut butter
coconut, optional

Thoroughly mix carob and milk powder into honey. Stir peanut butter into this. Form into balls by rolling portions between palms. Roll in coconut. Chill to make more firm.

BROWN RICE CRISPIE TREATS:
Leave out carob and add 1 1/2 cups Rice Crispies or Brown Rice Crisps. Press into pie pan. Chill then cut into bars.

TAHINI COOKIES

1/3 cup Tahini (sesame seed butter)
2/3 cup honey or brown rice syrup
1 1/2 cups quick oats

1/2 cup chopped NUTS OR SEEDS
1/4 teaspoon salt

Mix wet and dry ingredients separately then combine together. Let sit 10 minutes. Bake on oiled cookie sheet at 350 degrees for 10-13 minutes. or until light golden brown and soft to the touch. Let cool on pan 5 minutes before removing from pan. Makes 20.

FRUIT COOKIES

1 1/2 cups applesauce, mashed banana or DRIED FRUIT JAM
1/2 teaspoon salt
1 3/4 cups quick oats
1/4 cup whole grain flour

1/4 cup chopped NUTS OR SEEDS
1 teaspoon vanilla
1 1/2 cups chopped dried fruit

Stir together dry ingredients then combine with remaining items, stirring only enough to moisten oats. Shape into cookies. Bake on oiled cookie sheet at 350 degrees for 25-30 minutes. Makes 15-20.

PEANUT BUTTER COOKIES

1/4 cup honey
3/4 cup peanut butter

1/4 teaspoon salt
1 cup oat flour

Make oat flour by blending quick or rolled oats. Stir together all ingredients, adding the flour last. Roll into small balls the size of an unshelled walnut. Place on an oiled cookie sheet. Flatten with a fork, that is moistened with water, to about 1/4 inch thick. Bake at 350 degrees for 7-10 minutes, until golden brown. Makes 15-18.

GOLDEN MACAROONS

1 cup grated raw carrots, packed
1/2 cup water
1/2 cup SWEETENER pg 6
1 teaspoon vanilla

1 1/2 cups coconut
1 cup oat flour
1/2 teaspoon salt

Make oat flour by blending quick or rolled oats. Mix well all ingredients. Let sit 10 minutes. Firmly pack dough into a tablespoon then drop on an oiled cookie sheet. Bake at 350 degrees for 25 minutes.

OATMEAL RAISIN COOKIES

1 cup honey
3/4 cup water
2/3 cup oil
1/2 cup chopped NUTS OR SEEDS
1 1/2 cups raisins or carob chips

1 1/2 cups oat flour
1 teaspoon vanilla
1 1/2 teaspoons salt
1 1/2 teaspoons lemon extract
4 2/3 cups quick oats

Make oat flour by blending 1 1/2 cups quick or rolled oats. Stir together all ingredients except quick oats. Mix in remaining 4 2/3 cups of oats. Let dough sit 10 minutes. To shape the easiest way use a cookie scoop that holds about 2 tablespoons. Periodically moisten scoop to keep dough from sticking. Slightly flatten with a fork. Or use a metal serving spoon to put dough into to shape cookie. Moisten spoon as needed. Place on oiled cookie sheets. Bake at 350 degrees for 20 minutes or until light golden brown. Makes 3 dozen. Let cool 5 minutes before removing from cookie sheet.

BANANA ICE CREAM

Peel ripe, but not over ripe, bananas. Place in plastic bag and freeze solid. This takes several hours. To make ice cream cut 2 medium size frozen bananas into about 5 or 6 pieces. Place in blender. Blend with 1/2-3/4 cup liquid, or just enough to slowly turn bananas through the blades. The liquid may be fruit juice, juice concentrate, water, soy milk or nut milk. While blending use a rubber spatula to help bananas rotate. Turn off blender and stir as needed. Serve immediately or, to make more firm, put into freezer. Ice cream will keep in the freezer up to 1-2 hours, depending on the freezer, before getting to hard to serve. Use as dessert or over WAFFLES, PAN-CAKES, FRENCH TOAST, GRANOLA, cooked or dry cereal, etc.

CAROB MINT ICE CREAM

2 frozen bananas
1/2-3/4 cup water or soy milk
3 tablespoons nuts of choice

1 1/2 tablespoons carob powder
1/8 teaspoon peppermint extract
1/16 teaspoon salt

Follow directions for BANANA ICE CREAM, leaving out the liquid called for in that recipe.

MAPLE WALNUT ICE CREAM

2 frozen bananas
1/2-3/4 cup water or soy milk
3 tablespoons walnuts or pecans

1/2 teaspoon vanilla
1/8 teaspoon maple extract
1/16 teaspoon salt

Follow directions for BANANA ICE CREAM, leaving out the liquid called for in that recipe.

CAROB ICE CREAM

2 frozen bananas
1 tablespoon carob powder

1/2-3/4 cup soy milk

Follow directions for BANANA ICE CREAM, leaving out the liquid called for in that recipe.

BUTTERSCOTCH ICE CREAM

2 frozen bananas
1/2-3/4 cup water or soy milk
3 tablespoons nuts of choice

1/4 teaspoon butterscotch extract
1/16 teaspoon salt

Follow directions for BANANA ICE CREAM, leaving out the liquid called for in that recipe.

TOFU ICE CREAM

1/4 cup unsweetened juice concentrate of choice
1 cup frozen fruit of choice
1 frozen banana

1/4 cup tofu
soy milk or water, as needed

Blend smooth all ingredients. Use just enough soy milk or water to slowly turn fruit through blades.

CHAMPION ICE CREAM

Frozen bananas run through a Champion Juicer make a delicious ice cream. For other flavors of ice cream using the juicer try mixing other frozen fruits with frozen bananas. Bananas give creaminess. Other frozen fruits tend to give a more icy consistency but adding bananas with other fruit helps maintain a creamy texture.

BANANA BOATS

Peel banana, cut in half crosswise then coat with one of the following:

1. DRIED FRUIT JAM
2. CAROB PEANUT BUTTER FROSTING
3. EMULSIFIED PEANUT BUTTER OR TAHINI
4. HOMEMADE NUT OR SEED BUTTER

Roll coated banana in coconut. Place on a plate and freeze. When frozen serve as they are or for easier serving cut each section in half again and poke a toothpick in the center. Store left overs in a plastic bag in the freezer.

DRESSINGS, GRAVIES & SPREADS

HOW LONG DO THEY KEEP?

A big question is, "How long do these dressings and spreads keep?". Since they do not have preservatives in them, naturally they don't keep as long as commercial products, but much depends on you. With proper attention these items should last 11/2-2 weeks. (Ketchup and fruit spreads generally keep 2 -3 weeks.) Here are some helpful guidelines: (1) keep them in the refrigerator as much as possible; (2) refrigerate soon after preparation; (3) do not remove from refrigerator until it is time to eat; (4) put back in the refrigerator first thing after the meal (not after the dishes are done); (5) divide up recipe and put in serving containers which will likely be emptied after 3 or 4 days as each time the dish is taken out for meals will reduce its life span; (6) do not mix a more fresh recipe in the same serving dish as one that has been exposed to room temperature several times; (7) do not take the serving spoon from an older spread and use it in a fresh spread as the old one runs out; (8) if amount is more than will likely be used in 2 weeks, cut the recipe. Several of these gravies, spreads and dressings can be frozen. If using one that has been frozen use this procedure: Thaw recipe then place in sauce pan. Lightly boil, stirring, about three minutes, or until product has become smooth. Reblending is not usually necessary for smoothness. Chill to thicken spreads or dressings.

SUN SEED TOMATO DRESSING

1 1/4 cups canned tomatoes with juice

1/4 cup sunflower seeds	**1/8 teaspoon garlic powder**
2 tablespoons lemon juice	**1/2 teaspoon onion powder**
3/4 teaspoon salt	**1 teaspoon SWEETENER pg 6**

Blend together all ingredients until smooth. Add up to ¼ cup additional sunflower seeds if a thicker consistency is desired.

HUMMUS

1 cup cooked garbanzo beans	**1 garlic clove**
1/4 cup toasted sesame seeds	**1/4-1/2 teaspoon salt**
3 tablespoons lemon juice	**2-4 tablespoons water**

Toast seeds in a dry skillet on medium heat 5-10 minutes, stirring frequently, until golden brown. Blend all ingredients until smooth. Add 1/4 teaspoon of salt if the beans are salt free.

VARIATIONS:
1. Substitute 1/4 cup Tahini (sesame seed butter) for the seeds.
2. Substitute 1 tablespoon toasted sesame seed oil for the seeds. Less water will be needed.
3. For a dressing add 2-4 tablespoons water.

LOW-CAL FRENCH DRESSING

1/4 cup hot cooked rice or millet, cooked pasta or tofu

1 cup canned tomatoes	**1/8 teaspoon garlic powder**
1/4 teaspoon onion powder	**1 teaspoon lemon juice**
1 teaspoon SWEETENER pg 6	**1/8 teaspoon basil**
1/4 teaspoon salt	

Blend all ingredients smooth.

SUMMER SALAD DRESSING

1/2 cup mashed avocado	**1/4 teaspoon garlic powder**
3/4 cup water	**1 1/4 teaspoons onion powder**
1/4 cup cashews	**3/4 teaspoon salt**
2 tablespoons lemon juice	

Blend smooth all ingredients.

FRENCH TOMATO DRESSING

1/2 cup oil	**1/4 cup water**
2 tablespoons lemon juice	**1 teaspoon salt**
3 tablespoons tomato paste	**1/4 teaspoon onion powder**
2 tablespoons SWEETENER pg 6	

Blend smooth all ingredients.

QUICK CORN SAUCE

1 15 oz. can whole corn with juice	**1/2 teaspoon salt**
1/4 cup coconut	

Blend smooth all ingredients. Serve over winter squash, potatoes or other vegetable.

TASTY SESAME TOPPING

White or brown sesame seeds may be used. Toast seeds in a dry skillet over medium heat, stirring, 5-10 minutes until golden brown. Blend smooth all ingredients. Sprinkle over salads, vegetables, rice, beans, MACARONI AND CHEESE, PIZZA, SPAGHETTI, etc.

CREAMY LOW-CAL MAYONNAISE

1 1/4 cups water
1/4 cup white flour
1/4 cup cashews
1 1/2 tablespoons lemon juice

1/8 teaspoon garlic powder
1 teaspoon salt
1/2 teaspoon onion powder

Blend smooth all ingredients. Empty into a sauce pan and lightly boil, stirring, until thickened. Chill.

TOFU MAYONNAISE

1 package 12.3 oz. Firm or Extra Firm Mori-Nu Tofu
1/4 cup soy milk powder, optional
1 tablespoon lemon juice
1/2 teaspoon onion powder

3/4 teaspoon salt
2 tablespoons oil, optional
1/8 teaspoon garlic powder

Blend smooth all ingredients. Chill.

SUN SEED SPREAD

1/2 cup sunflower seeds
1/2 cup hot, cooked rice, millet or cooked pasta
3/4 cup water
1/4 teaspoon dill weed or seed
1 1/2 teaspoons onion powder

1/2-1 teaspoon salt

1/2 teaspoon garlic powder
2 tablespoons lemon juice

Blend all until smooth. Serve on crackers, bread, as a vegetable dip or as a sour cream for baked potatoes. May add 2 tablespoons of water while blending to make a dressing.

YEASTY SPREAD

1/2 cup SUN SEED SPREAD or MAYONNAISE
2 tablespoons YEAST FLAKES pg 6

Stir ingredients together well. Spread over bread or crackers, as a salad dip, or on baked potatoes.

BEAN SPREAD

1 cup cooked beans, i.e. soybeans   1/4 cup dressing of choice

Mash or blend beans with the dressing. Try MAYONNAISE, CHEESE SAUCE or SPREAD, SUNSEED TOMATO DRESSING or SUN SEED SPREAD.

AVOCADO BUTTER

3/4 cup mashed avocado
1 tablespoon lemon juice
1/2 teaspoon onion powder

1/8 teaspoon salt
1/8 teaspoon garlic powder

Combine all and serve in a sandwich with tomato slices and alfalfa sprouts.

KETCHUP

6 oz. can of tomato paste
6 oz. or 2/3 cup water
2 tablespoons lemon juice
1/4 teaspoon salt

3/4 teaspoon onion powder
1/4 teaspoon basil
1/4 teaspoon dill weed
1/4 teaspoon garlic powder

Mix well.

PESTO

1 cup packed fresh basil leaves, approximately 2 ounces
1/2 cup TOASTED walnuts pg 63   1 tablespoon lemon juice
1/4 teaspoon salt   1/4 cup water
2 cloves garlic   2 tablespoon YEAST FLAKES, opt

Blend all until smooth.

MILLET BUTTER

1 cup hot, cooked millet, packed   1 cup water
1/3 cup coconut or cashews   1 teaspoon salt

Blend all until very smooth. Add a small amount of water while blending if necessary. If millet is cold to begin with it can be heated with water from the recipe then blended.

VARIATIONS:
1. Add 1/4 cup cooked carrots while blending for color.
2. OR Add 1/16 teaspoon of turmeric while blending for color.
3. Add 1/16 teaspoon of butter extract while blending for flavor.
4. For a lighter spread that softens when placed on hot food leave out 1/3 cup millet. Heat water in a sauce pan. Add all ingredients plus 1 tablespoon Emes Plain Kosher Jel to blender. Blend smooth. Chill.

FRESH CORN BUTTER

1 1/2 cups fresh or frozen corn   **2-4 tablespoons water**
1/2 teaspoon salt   **3 tablespoons coconut, optional**

Cook corn. Blend all smooth. Serve over bread, corn on the cob, vegetables.

EMULSIFIED NUT BUTTER

1/2 cup peanut butter or nut butter of choice
1/4 cup water or juice   **1/2 cup crushed pineapple,**
1/4 cup additional water or juice   **optional**

Stir with a fork the nut butter and water or juice. Add pineapple and mix well. Add as much additional liquid as needed to make butter creamy and easy to spread but not runny. Store in refrigerator.

NUT OR SEED BUTTER

1 cup NUTS OR SEEDS pg 6   **1/4 teaspoon salt**
1/2 cup water   **1/4-1/2 cup additional water**

Blend smooth, if possible, all but additional water. Add as much from the additional water as needed to turn the nuts in the blades and make it smooth. Some nuts require more water than others. Store in refrigerator.

CAROB MILLET SAUCE

1 cup hot, cooked millet   **1 teaspoon vanilla**
1-2 tablespoons carob powder   **1/4 teaspoon salt**
2 tablespoons peanut butter   **3/4 cup water**
1 1/2 tablespoons SWEETENER   **1 banana**

Blend all until smooth. Chill.

VARIATIONS:
1. Leave out banana and sweetener. Add 2 tablespoons of mild molasses.
2. Substitute 3 tablespoons of cashews for the peanut butter.

APPLE BUTTER

4 cups apple sauce
1 teaspoon vanilla

1/2 teaspoon coriander

Mix all and pour into flat baking pan 1 inch deep. Bake at 350 degrees for 1 hour, or until desired consistency. Stir occasionally during baking.

DRIED FRUIT JAM

1 1/4 cups chopped dried fruit

1 cup water or fruit juice of choice

Bring ingredients to a light boil in a covered sauce pan. Turn off heat. Let sit 5-10 minutes. Blend smooth.

VARIATIONS:
1. Combine equal amounts of dates and apricots with pineapple juice.
2. Add 1/2 teaspoon dried orange peel, 1/4 teaspoon coriander, 1/2 teaspoon vanilla to prune or date jam.
3. Blend 1/4 cup fresh, canned or frozen (drained) fruit while blending jam. Try apple, banana, peach or grapes.

FRUIT SPREAD

1 cup fruit juice
2 tablespoons cornstarch

1/3 cup DRIED FRUIT JAM
1/3 cup crushed pineapple

Lightly boil juice and starch together, stirring 5 minutes, until thickened. Stir in remaining ingredients. Chill.

VARIATIONS:
1. Use 1/2 cup juice concentrate and 1/2 cup water in place of fruit juice.
2. Use other crushed or mashed fruit such as berries, grapes, peaches.

FRUIT SAUCE

Follow FRUIT SPREAD recipe but reduce cornstarch to 1 tablespoon.

Serve warm over WAFFLES, PANCAKES, GRANOLA, or cooked cereal. Chill and serve over MILLET PUDDING or TOFU CHEESE CAKE.

STRAWBERRY JAM

1 cup strawberries
2-4 tablespoons SWEETENER pg 6

1/2 teaspoon vanilla
1 tablespoon granulated tapioca

Strawberries may be fresh or frozen. Frozen berries should be thawed, drained and equal to 1 cup drained. Blend all ingredients until smooth. Lightly boil until tapioca is clear, stirring. Chill. (See page 64 for canning directions.)

VARIATIONS:
1. Use 1/4 cup unsweetened juice concentrate in place of sweetener.
2. Use other fruits such as grapes, other berries and peaches.

WATERMELON JAM

Do you have a bumper crop of watermelons? Remove rind and hard seeds then blend the melon. Cook it down in an open pot for a few hours to desired consistency, stirring occasionally. Make as a sauce or cook down more to a jam. Add 1/2 teaspoon vanilla per 2 cups watermelon after cooked.

AVOCADO PINEAPPLE SPREAD

mashed avocado
mashed banana

crushed pineapple

Stir together equal amounts of each item.

CHICKEN STYLE GRAVY

1/2 cup water
1/2 cup cashews
1/4 cup cornstarch
2 tablespoons CHICKEN STYLE SEASONING pg 63

1 1/2 teaspoons onion powder
1 teaspoon salt
4 cups addition water

Blend smooth all but additional water. Pour blended ingredients into a sauce pan. Rinse blender with the additional water, pour into pan. Lightly boil, stirring about 10 minutes, until thickened.

HERB GRAVY

1/2 cup water
1/2 cup cashews
1/3 cup YEAST FLAKES, optional
1/4 cup cornstarch
1 tablespoon onion powder

2 teaspoons salt
1/4 teaspoon basil
1/2 teaspoon garlic powder
1/8 teaspoon oregano
4 cups additional water

Blend smooth all but additional water. Pour blended ingredients into a sauce pan. Rinse blender with the additional water, pour into pan. Lightly boil, stirring about 10 minutes, until thickened.

PEANUT BUTTER GRAVY

1/2 cup water
1/3 cup peanut butter or other nut butter
1/4 cup cornstarch

2 teaspoons salt

4 cups additional water

Blend smooth all but additional water. Pour blended ingredients into a sauce pan. Rinse blender with the additional water, pour into pan. Lightly boil, stirring about 10 minutes, until thickened.

WHITE SAUCE

1/2 cup water
1/2 cup cashews
1/4 cup cornstarch

2 teaspoons salt
1 1/2 teaspoons onion powder
4 cups additional water

Blend smooth all but additional water. Pour blended ingredients into a sauce pan. Rinse blender with the additional water, pour into pan. Lightly boil, stirring about 10 minutes, until thickened.

ENTREES

MEAL PLANNING IDEAS

Loaves, patties and casseroles are enjoyable to have but are not essential for adequate nutrition. Similar nutrients are available in peas, beans, potatoes, winter squash, served with bread, corn, rice and other similar quick and easy items. To make a simple, tasty meal keep on hand 2 or 3 kinds of dressings, gravies, or sauces to serve over beans, rice, etc.

CHEAPER NUTS

Nut meal (nuts already ground) can be used in any recipe where the nuts are blended up (dressing, gravy, entree, milk). Nuts in this form are generally cheaper. Buy at groceries or health food stores. Food co-ops and bulk food stores usually have best prices. Buy in bulk, freeze.

TOFU LOAF

1 pound or 2 cups firm or extra firm tofu
3 cups flake cereal i.e. Corn Flakes or whole grain flake cold cereal
2 cups blended bread crumbs   **1 cup water**
1 chopped onion   **1 1/2 teaspoons salt**
2/3 cup chopped celery   **1 1/4 teaspoons basil**
2/3 cup chopped nuts   **1/2 teaspoon sage**

Break up one slice of whole grain bread into 5 pieces. Place in blender and blend until fine. Repeat this step to make 2 cups. If using a food processor to make crumbs more bread can be ground at a time. Coarsely crush flake cereal in a food processor or put cereal in a plastic bag and crush by hand or with a rolling pin. Mash tofu with a fork or potato masher. Combine all ingredients and place in an 8x8 oiled dish. Cover and bake at 350 degrees for 20 minutes. Uncover and bake as is for 20 minutes or add one or more of the Toppings listed. (If doubling the recipe use a 9 1/2 x 15 dish. Cover and bake 30 minutes. Uncover and bake additional 30 minutes.)

Toppings:
1. Drizzle with BASIC CHEESE SAUCE, TENDER LOW-CAL CHEESE or tomato sauce.
2. SHREDDED AGAR CHEESE or SHREDDED TOFU CHEESE looks attractive sprinkled on loaf with tomato sauce or BASIC CHEESE SAUCE drizzled on during the last 20 minutes of baking.

PECAN LOAF

1 1/4 cups pecans	1 cup water
2 cups cooked brown rice	1 1/2 teaspoons salt
4 cups blended bread crumbs	1 teaspoon basil
1 onion, quartered	

Break up one slice of whole grain bread into 5 pieces. Place in blender and blend until fine. Repeat this step to make 4 cups. If using a food processor to make crumbs more bread can be ground at a time. Place onion, 1/2 cup of the pecans and the water in blender and blend smooth. Remove from blender and mix together with rice and bread crumbs. Chop remaining 3/4 cup of pecans and add to mixture and mix well.

For MEATBALLS: Form balls by hand. Or use a cookie or ice cream scoop that hold 2-4 tablespoons. Pack the mixture into a scoop then place on oiled cookie sheet. The scoop method goes very quickly. Bake 30 minutes at 350 degrees. Reheat with spaghetti sauce or gravy in a flat baking dish.

For PATTIES: Shape patties about 1/2 inch thick. Bake on an oiled cookie sheet at 350 degrees for 30 minutes. Turn patties over and continue baking 10-15 minutes.
OR shape patties 1/4 inch thick. Fry in a lightly oiled non-stick fry pan approximately 15 minutes over medium heat. Brown both sides.

For LOAF: Pack into an oiled 8x8 dish. Cover and bake at 350 degrees for 30 minutes. Uncover and continue to bake 15 minutes.
Ways to serve: hot with gravy, cold loaf slices in a sandwich or use to make a sandwich spread by crumbling loaf and adding a spread, ketchup or cheese sauce for moistness. Good for sack lunch.

Leftover loaf, patties and meatballs freeze well.

VARIATIONS:
1. Use cooked millet in place of rice.
2. Use other nuts or seeds for pecans. Walnuts are very good.
3. Add 1 pound of mashed tofu while mixing ingredients.
4. During the last 15 minutes of baking the loaf drizzle tomato sauce and/ or BASIC CHEESE SAUCE on top.
5. SHREDDED AGAR CHEESE or SHREDDED TOFU CHEESE also looks attractive sprinkled on loaf with tomato sauce drizzled on during the last 15 minutes of baking.
6. Reheat with gravy on top of loaf or with a layer of ketchup or spaghetti sauce.

LOW-FAT PATTIES

4 cups cooked millet or rice	1 cup water
2 cups blended bread crumbs	1 1/2 teaspoons salt
2/3 cup NUTS OR SEEDS pg 6	1 teaspoon basil
1 onion, chopped	1/2 teaspoon sage or thyme

Break up one slice of whole grain bread into 5 pieces. Place in blender and blend until fine. Repeat this step to make 2 cups. If using a food processor to make crumbs more bread can be ground at a time. Chop onion and nuts or seeds. Mix together all ingredients.

See PECAN LOAF for ways to prepare as meatballs, patties or a loaf. VARIATIONS #4-6 under PECAN LOAF may be used for this recipe.

MILLET TOMATO LOAF

1 cup uncooked millet	1/2 teaspoon sage
1 cup tomato juice	1/2 teaspoon savory or marjoram
1 onion, quartered	3 cups additional tomato juice
1/2 cup cashews	1/2 cup chopped olives, optional
1/2 teaspoon salt	

In a 2 quart casserole combine additional juice with millet and olives. Blend smooth remaining ingredients. Stir into casserole. Cover, bake at 350 degrees for 75 minutes. Remove from oven, take lid off and let set 10 minutes before serving.

COOKING CHART FOR BEANS

BEANS (SOAKED)	INCHES OF WATER TO COVER TOP OF BEANS	APPROXIMATE COOKING TIME
Lentils, Split Peas, Mung Beans*	1 inch	1 hour
Black, Kidney, Baby Lima, Pinto, Navy Beans	2 inch	2-3 hours
Garbanzo (Chick Peas), Soybeans	3 inch	4-5 hours

Rinse beans then cover with 3 times more water than beans, soak 8 hours then drain. Skip soaking lentils, split peas, mung beans. Cover beans with fresh water. See chart for amount of water to use. Lightly boil in a covered pan. More water may eventually be needed. Do not add salt until beans are tender. Add 1 tsp. salt per 4 cups beans. 1 cup dry beans equal about 2 1/2 cups cooked. *No soaking needed for this group. Old soy beans may only get tender by cooking in a crock pot or pressure cooking or canning.

OATBURGERS

1/4 cup toasted sesame seeds	2 teaspoons salt
4 1/2 cups quick or rolled oats	1 teaspoon basil
1 cup water	1 1/2 teaspoons dill seed
1 onion, quartered	1 teaspoon oregano
1/4 cup sunflower seeds	2 garlic cloves OR
1/4 cup YEAST FLAKES pg 6	1 teaspoon garlic powder
3 cups additional boiling water	

Toast sesame seeds in a dry skillet over medium heat, stirring 5 minutes, until golden brown. Bring the 3 cups of additional water to a boil. While doing this blend smooth all remaining ingredients, except the oats and sesame seeds, with the 1 cup of water. Mix all ingredients together into the boiling water continuing to stir for one minute. Remove from heat and let sit 15 minutes. Form into patties 1/2 inch thick. Place on oiled cookie sheet. Bake at 350 degrees for 30 minutes, flip and bake an additional 10 minutes. Make 15-20.

Ways to serve: Place a single layer of burgers or meatballs in a casserole and top with gravy or spaghetti sauce. OR serve hot or cold in a sandwich with mayonnaise, ketchup and sprouts.

VARIATION:
1. Burgers may be shaped into meatballs. Bake for 30-35 minutes.
2. Substitute toasted sesame seeds for other NUTS OR SEEDS, page 6.
3. Add 1 pound of mashed tofu when mixing all the ingredients together.

GARBANZO RICE PATTIES

1 1/4 cups soaked garbanzo beans	3 tablespoons Yeast Flakes, opt.
1 1/2 cups cooked rice	1/4 teaspoon salt
3/4 cup water	1/2 teaspoon onion powder
1/3 cup chopped NUTS OR SEEDS	1/8 teaspoon garlic powder
2 teaspoons CHICKEN STYLE SEASONING pg 63 or 1/2 teaspoon salt	

Rinse 1/2 cup dry garbanzo beans, cover with 2 cups water. Soak about 8 hours. Drain. Blend beans and water until fairly smooth. Mix all ingredients in a bowl, form into patties 1/2 inch thick. Bake on an oiled cookie sheet at 350 degrees for 30 minutes, flip and bake an additional 10 minutes.

ROLL UPS

Take any cooked loaf or patty of choice. Crumble then add a moist dressing, spread, mayonnaise, ketchup or sauce to desired consistency. This mixture may be heated or used cold. Roll up in warm or room temperature whole grain soft tortillas. May add alfalfa sprouts to the roll up.
Other recipes that are good in roll ups include: SPANISH RICE, any mashed bean dish such as EASY BEANS made with soybeans, or refried beans.

SUN SEED ROAST

1 1/2 cups quick or rolled oats	3 tablespoons YEAST FLAKES
3/4 cup hot water	1/2 teaspoon thyme
3/4 cup sunflower seeds	1 3/4 teaspoons salt
1 onion, quartered	2 cups or 1# firm tofu, mashed
1/2 cup cracked wheat	3 cups additional water

Blend smooth all but oats, tofu, cracked wheat and additional water. Combine all ingredients. Pour into an oiled 2 quart casserole. Cover and bake at 350 degrees for 40 minutes. Uncover and bake 15 additional minutes.

VARIATIONS:
1. Substitute walnuts or other NUTS AND SEEDS for sunflower seeds.
2. Chop nuts instead of blending.

GRILLED CHEESE

Spread a thin layer of MILLET BUTTER on both sides of bread slices or leave it off. Lay on plate. Slice AGAR CHEESE 1/4 inch thick and place on bread or use 1/4 inch of CHEESE SPREAD. Add thin slice of onion and tomato, if desired, then top with bread. Grill in non-stick pan on medium low heat until golden brown on each side. Also may broil open face sandwiches on a cookie sheet.

SPANISH RICE

3 cups cooked rice	1 cup chopped onions
1 1/4 cups canned tomatoes	1/2 cup chopped green pepper
2/3 cup tomato paste	1 teaspoon basil
1 cup cooked garbanzo beans	1/2 teaspoon salt

Simmer, until vegetables are tender, all ingredients but rice and beans. Add rice and beans. Heat and serve or bake, uncovered, 30 minutes at

350 degees. Baking will help recipe to set more firmly.

CARROT RICE CASSEROLE

2 cups cooked rice	1 2/3 cups water
2 cups finely grated carrots	1 1/2 teaspoons salt
1 cup blended bread crumbs	1 teaspoon onion powder
1/2 cup chopped onions	1/2 teaspoon garlic powder
1/3 cup peanut butter or other	1/4 teaspoon thyme
nut butter of choice	

Break up one slice of whole grain bread into 5 pieces. Place in blender and blend until fine. Repeat to make 1 cup. Dissolve nut butter into water. Mix all ingredients together. Bake in oiled 2 quart casserole, covered, at 350 degrees for 40 minutes. Uncover and continue baking 10 minutes.

MACARONI AND CHEESE

3 cups cooked macaroni
2 cups TENDER LOW-CAL CHEESE pg 27

Make the cheese using the variation of substituting 3 tablespoons of oil for the cashews. This will make a nicer consistency when heating recipe in the oven as nuts in the cheese tend to give a curdled look when baked with pasta. If heating on stove top use either the nuts or oil in the cheese.

SPAGHETTI SAUCE

4 cups canned tomatoes	1 tablespoon honey
1 1/2 cups tomato paste	2 teaspoons basil
1 1/2 cups chopped onions	3/4 teaspoon salt
1/2 cup green pepper	1/2 teaspoon marjoram
1-2 minced garlic cloves	1/2 teaspoon oregano

Combine all ingredients. Simmer 20 minutes. Sauce may be blended after cooking for a smooth sauce.

PIZZA

For the crust use 1 recipe of BASIC WHOLE WHEAT BREAD dough. Reduce yeast to 1 teaspoon. Roll out dough on oiled cookie sheet. Cover with 2 1/2 cups of spaghetti sauce then add any of the following Pizza Toppings. Bake at 350 degrees for 35-40 minutes.

Pizza Topping:
1. Drizzle on BASIC CHEESE SAUCE or TENDER LOW-CAL CHEESE.
2. May sprinkle the following on tomato sauce before the cheese is added: crumbled, baked PECAN LOAF or LOW-FAT PATTIES.
3. Sliced olives, peppers or onions may also be added.

LASAGNA

lasagna noodles, 3/4-1 pound **1 pound or 2 cups tofu, mashed**
7 cups spaghetti sauce **cheese sauce**

Noodles may be cooked first or left uncooked. The lasagna comes out delicious either way but it is easier to assemble if noodles are uncooked. Layer in a 9 1/2x13 1/2 oiled dish as follows: 2 cups sauce on bottom of dish, noodles that slightly overlap, 1 1/2 cups sauce and 1 cup mashed tofu, noodles, 1 1/2 cups sauce, tofu, noodles, and ending with remaining sauce. Cover dish and bake at 350 degrees for 45 minutes. Remove from oven and poke noodles with a knife to see in they are soft. If not then cover and bake an additional 10-15 minutes. Uncover and adding Lasagna Toppings of choice and continue to bake 15 minutes.

LASAGNA TOPPINGS:
1. Drizzle with BASIC CHEESE SAUCE or TENDER LOW-CAL CHEESE.
2. Top with SHREDDED AGAR CHEESE or SHREDDED TOFU CHEESE.
3. Add sliced olives on top before baking the lasagna.

VARIATIONS:
1. Mix 3/4 cup MAYONNAISE with the mashed tofu.
2. Crumble some baked loaf or patty and sprinkle on top of the tofu layers.

SPAGHETTI & MEATBALLS

cooked spaghetti **meatballs**
spaghetti sauce **cheese sauce**

Heat spaghetti sauce with meatballs. Meatballs may be made from PECAN LOAF, LOW-FAT PATTIES or OATBURGERS. Serve over cooked pasta. Top with BASIC CHEESE SAUCE or TENDER LOW-CAL CHEESE and/or SHREDDED CHEESE, or TASTY SESAME TOPPING.

SAVORY BEANS & RICE

2 cans 15.5 oz. beans or 3 1/2 cups **2 bay leaves**

1/2 cup chopped onion

1/2 cup chopped green pepper

1 chopped garlic clove

1 1/2 teaspoons onion powder

1 tablespoon cumin

Cook vegetables and bay leaves in a covered sauce pan in a small amount of water until done. Do not drain the canned beans. Mix all ingredients in sauce pan and heat to serve. Serve over brown rice.

BAKED BEANS

6 cups cooked beans, i.e. soys, or 1 jar 48 oz. Randles beans, drained

1 can 15 oz. chopped tomatoes or stewed tomatoes

2 chopped garlic cloves

1/4 cup mild molasses

1 chopped onion

Cook onion and garlic in a covered sauce pan with a small amount of water until done. Mix all ingredients together. Bake at 350 degrees, uncovered, for 45-60 minutes or to desired consistency.

EASY BEANS

6 cups cooked beans, i.e. soys, or 1 jar 48 oz. Randles beans, drained

2 cups spaghetti sauce

Mix ingredients and bake at 350 degrees, uncovered, 30 minutes or until desired consistency. Baking can be left out but beans will be more runny. This more runny consistency is good served over rice, potatoes, pasta.

HAY STACKS

CHEESE SAUCE or TENDER LOW-CAL CHEESE and/or MAYONNAISE

EASY BEANS, SAVORY BEANS or beans of choice

Oil-free Corn Chips

Place chips on plate. Spoon on beans. Add any of the following: SPROUTS, tomato, lettuce, onion, pepper, cucumber, blanched broccoli, etc. Top with cheese sauce and/or mayonnaise.

CHICKPEA A LA KING

3/4 cup water

1/2 cup cashews

3 tablespoons CHICKEN STYLE SEASONING pg 63

1 teaspoon salt

1/4 cup flour

1/2 cup chopped onion   1 1/2 cups frozen green peas
2 1/4 cups additional water   2/3 cup sliced carrots
1 1/2 cups cooked garbanzo beans or 15 oz. can, drained

Blend smooth nuts, seasonings and flour with the 3/4 water. Pour into a sauce pan. Rinse blender with the additional water and pour into pan. Lightly boil, stirring, until thickened. In a separate pan cook carrots and onions in small amount of water until tender. Add peas, cook an additional 3 minutes. Combine all and heat. Serve over rice, noodles or potatoes.

SCRAMBLED TOFU

1 pound or 2 cups firm or extra firm tofu (Mori-Nu or water packed)
2 teaspoons CHICKEN STYLE SEASONING pg 63
1/4 teaspoon garlic powder   1/4 teaspoon turmeric (for color)
1/2 teaspoon salt   1 1/2 tablespoons YEAST FLAKES
1 1/2 teaspoons onion powder   2 teaspoons oil, optional

Mash tofu with a fork or potato masher. Heat all ingredients together in a nonstick fry pan or sauce pan. Eat as is or with KETCHUP, BASIC CHEESE SAUCE or TENDER LOW-CAL CHEESE. Serve with a fruit meal, vegetable meal or as a sandwich filling.

VARIATIONS:
1. Sauté chopped onion, green pepper and/or garlic in oil or small amount of water before adding the recipe ingredients.
2. Substitute 2 teaspoons toasted sesame seed oil for oil.
3. Add 1/4 teaspoon liquid Smoked Hickory flavoring while heating.

BAKED TOFU

1 pound tofu (Mori-Nu or water packed)

Cut tofu in 1/4 inch thick slices. Season on both sides as desired. Sprinkle with any of the following: granulated garlic or onion, salt, CHICKEN STYLE SEASONING, herbs or other favorite seasoning or dip in breading meal. Bake at 350 degrees on an oiled cookie sheet. Flip after 15 minutes and continue to bake 15 minutes or until desired chewiness. Serve as is, in a sandwich or topped with gravy.

VARIATION:
Fry in a nonstick fry pan instead of bake. Fry over medium heat 10 minutes, flip and continue 5 minutes or until golden brown and chewy.

CHIPPED TOFU WITH VEGIES

Prepare BAKED TOFU then cut into bite size pieces. Add baked tofu to 1 recipe of WHITE SAUCE or CHICKEN STYLE GRAVY and 4 1/2 cups of cooked vegetables of choice. Reheat and serve over rice, pasta or potatoes.

TOFU PATTIES

1 pound or 2 cups firm or extra firm tofu (Mori-Nu or water packed)
2 teaspoons salt   2 tablespoon YEAST FLAKES, opt
3 1/2 cups quick or rolled oats   1/2 teaspoon marjoram
1 3/4 cups water   1/4 teaspoon thyme
1 onion, quartered   2 garlic cloves

Blend all ingredients smooth except the oats. Stir in oats and let sit 10 minutes. Bake patties on an oiled cookie sheet at 350 degrees for 25 minutes. Flip and bake an additional 10-15 minutes. OR fry the patties on a lightly oiled nonstick fry pan. May also make meatballs and bake 30-35 minutes.

TOFU VEGETABLE QUICHE

1 box 12.3 oz firm or extra firm Mori-Nu or 1 1/2 cups water packed tofu
1/4 cup cornstarch   1 1/4 teaspoons salt
2/3 cup water   2 teaspoons cumin
1/4 cup YEAST FLAKES pg 6   1/2 teaspoon basil
1 onion, quartered   2 cups chopped vegetables
1 garlic clove

Blend smooth all but vegetables. Cook vegetables. May want to try water chestnuts, broccoli, pimento pieces, carrots or frozen mixed vegetables. Red and green colors are pretty. Stir all together. Place WHOLE WHEAT PIE CRUST in oiled 9 inch pie pan. Pour in filling. Bake at 350 degrees for 50 minutes. OR bake without a crust for 45 minutes in oiled pie pan.

POTATO WEDGES

Scrub potatoes, cut in half then cut in 4-6 wedges per half depending on the size of the potato. Rub 2 teaspoons of olive oil on a 10x15 cookie sheet. Cover with a single layer of potato wedges. Sprinkle with salt. Bake at 425 degrees for 30 minutes or until baked. Turn after 15 minutes. Serve with ketchup, cheese sauce, gravy or plain.

SCALLOPED POTATOES

8 cups sliced potatoes   **1 recipe WHITE SAUCE (less 1/2 cup water)**

Clean and peel potatoes. Slice 1/8 inch. Put potatoes and 3 1/2 cups of water in a large, flat sauce pan. Boil to partially cooked, 7-10 minutes. Drain potatoes and put into 9 1/2x13 1/2 baking dish. Make one recipe of WHITE SAUCE, leaving out 1/2 cup of the water, and pour over potatoes. Cover dish with foil. Bake at 400 degrees for 30 minutes. Uncover and bake an additional 20 minutes. Serve as is or drizzle with 1-2 cups BASIC CHEESE SAUCE or TENDER LOW-CAL CHEESE during the last 20 minutes of baking.

VEGETABLE POT PIE

1 1/2 cups cubed firm tofu or cubed BAKED TOFU
1/2 cup chopped onion   **2 1/2 cups gravy of choice**
1 cup diced carrots   **1 cup green peas**
1 cup diced potatoes   **WHOLE WHEAT PIE CRUST**

Cook vegetables until tender in small amount of water. Stir in tofu and gravy. If desiring a bottom crust use a double recipe for the crust and lightly oil a 1 1/2 quart casserole. Cover bottom and sides with portion of crust. Fill with vegetable mixture and top with remaining crust. Poke a few holes in the crust then bake at 350 degrees for 50 minutes.

VARIATIONS:
1. Use any cooked, dried bean or pea for green peas.
2. Substitute other vegetables such as frozen mixed vegetables.
3. Roll out BASIC WHOLE WHEAT BREAD dough 1/8 inch thick for the crust. Reduce the yeast to 1 teaspoon for dough. Bake as directed above.

HASH BROWNS

2 1/2 cups cooked potatoes, diced   1/4 teaspoon salt
2 teaspoons oil

Sauté all ingredients until lightly browned. Serve as is or with KETCHUP, BASIC CHEESE SAUCE or TENDER LOW-CAL CHEESE.

STUFFED PEPPERS OR ZUCCHINI OR CABBAGE ROLLS

Wash medium size peppers, cut off tops, remove seeds and parboil in salted water 3-5 minutes. Or wash medium size, 8" zucchini, cut off stem tip, cut in half length-wise. Scoop out center, leaving a thin shell. Parboil the same as the peppers. Or blanch cabbage leaves 3-5 minutes.

Stuff with one of the following unbaked mixes from the entree section (portion removed from zucchini may be added to the stuffing). For cabbage fill with 2-3 tablespoons. Fillings to try: TOFU LOAF, LOW-FAT PATTIES, PECAN LOAF or SPANISH RICE.

Top with 2-3 tablespoons of BASIC CHEESE SAUCE, GOLDEN SAUCE, or TENDER LOW-CAL CHEESE. Pour spaghetti sauce and or cheese sauce over cabbage. Try sprinkling with SHREDDED AGAR CHEESE or SHREDDED TOFU CHEESE over peppers, zucchini or cabbage. Bake, covered, at 350 degrees for 35-45 minutes.

ENCHILADAS

Fill whole wheat or corn tortillas with 1/4 cup SPANISH RICE, mashed beans, such as soybeans, or low fat refried beans. Tortillas should be at room temperature for easy folding. Roll. Pour 1 2/3 cups spaghetti sauce on bottom of 9 1/2x13 1/2 baking dish. Place 9 filled tortillas, seam side down, in dish. Top with 1 1/3 cups spaghetti sauce. Drizzle on 2/3 cup BASIC CHEESE SAUCE or TENDER LOW-CAL CHEESE. May want to put sliced olives and/or SHREDDED AGAR CHEESE or SHREDDED TOFU CHEESE on top of sauce. Bake at 350 degrees for 35 minutes.

VARIATION: Add 1 tablespoon of cumin to the spaghetti sauce.

QUICK BEAN PATTIES

1 1/2 cups cooked beans i.e. soys	**1 1/4 cups oat flour**
1/2 cup chopped NUTS OR SEEDS	**1/4 cup water**
1 onion, quartered	**1 tablespoon cumin**
3/4 teaspoon salt	**1/2 teaspoon sage**

Beans in this recipe are not salt free. Blend oats until fine then empty into a bowl. Blend smooth onion, beans and water. Mix all ingredients. Shape into patties. Bake at 350 degrees for 30 minutes, flip and bake an additional 10 minutes.

Of These...

58 - baked beans
58 - easy beans
60 - potato wedges
79 - split pea chowder

MISCELLANEOUS

CHICKEN STYLE SEASONING

1 1/3 cups YEAST FLAKES pg 6
3 tablespoons onion powder
2 1/2 teaspoons garlic powder
2 1/2 tablespoons salt

1/2 teaspoon celery seed
2 tablespoons Italian seasoning
1 teaspoon tumeric, for color
2 tablespoons parsley flakes

Blend smooth all except dry parsley flakes. Stir parsley in. Store in glass container. Avoid holding jar over steaming food as seasoning will take on moisture and become caked and stiff.

TOASTED NUTS AND SEEDS

Most nuts and seeds can be toasted on top of the stove in a skillet or sauce pan (do not use a nonstick pan), stirring continually. OR, in the oven on a cookie sheet stirring occasionally. The following instructions are using a sauce pan on the stove. Use a thin layer of nuts. Other nuts can be done with this method but the time and heat will vary with the nut.

Walnuts: Heat over med-low heat for 5-10 minutes, stirring.
Sesame Seeds: Heat over med-high heat for 5-10 minutes, stirring.
Coconut: Heat over med-low heat for 5 minutes, stirring.

SOY BASE

2 cups water
1 cup soy flour

1 teaspoon salt

Blend or stir all until smooth. After cooking, base should be custard consistency. Methods of cooking:

1. In oven in an uncovered dish at 350 degrees for 50 minutes, stirring after 20 minutes.
2. On top of stove using a simmer ring or heat deflector under a covered sauce pan. Cook on medium/low, stirring occasionally, for 30 minutes.
3. In a double boiler, covered, stirring occasionally. Cook for 2 hours.
4. In covered crock pot on medium (use low if pot has no medium) for about 3 hours or until thickened. Stir occasionally.

Soy base will keep in refrigerator a few days or may be frozen. Freezing in 1/2 cup proportions in plastic bags is convenient for many recipes.

SOAKED BEANS

Sort dried beans and cover with three times as much water and soak about 8 hours. Drain. May be stored in refrigerator 4-6 days or frozen in plastic bags. 1 cup dry beans will produce 2-2 1/2 cups soaked beans. The volume will change very little after the beans are cooked.

ORANGE PEEL

Save unsprayed orange peel (pesticide-free). Dry in the oven on a cookie sheet at lowest temperature possible or dry in a food dryer. Blend fine when dry. Store in a glass container. May keep in the freezer for longer shelf life.

BLENDED BREAD CRUMBS

Break up one slice of whole grain bread into 5 pieces. Blend fine. If using a food processor more bread can be done at a time to make crumbs.

CANNING IDEAS

Can the following recipes using the hot water bath method, boiling for 30 minutes. The recipes should be cooked if the oroginal directions for the recipe call for this.

KETCHUP   **APPLE BUTTER**
STRAWBERRY JAM   **FRUIT SPREAD**
DRIED FRUIT JAM   **WATERMELON JAM**

CANNED BEANS

1 2/3 cups dried beans or peas   1 teaspoon salt

Do not soak beans in water over night for this method. Place washed, sorted legumes, add salt if desired, in a quart jar. Fill with water to an inch from the top. Stir. Prepare lids as usual for canning. Pressure can at 10 lbs. for 90 minutes.

NOTE: This is an especially great way to cook garbanzo beans and soy beans as they tend to be difficult to get tender on the stove in a sauce pan.

NIGHTSHADES

NIGHTSHADE REPLACEMENTS

Many arthritics and those with other types of joint pain are sensitive to the nightshade family (tomato, white potato, hot and sweet peppers, eggplant and tobacco). For those individuals these recipes are added.

UN-TOMATO KETCHUP

1 cup cooked carrots
2 tablespoons cooked beets
1/4 cup water
4 teaspoons lemon juice
1 1/2 teaspoons SWEETENER pg 6

1/2 teaspoon salt
1/2 teaspoon onion powder
1/4 teaspoon garlic powder
1/4 teaspoon basil
1 teaspoon cumin

Blend smooth all ingredients.

UN-FRENCH DRESSING

1/3 cup cooked carrots
1 1/2 tablespoons cooked beets
3/4 cup water
2 tablespoons lemon juice
1/3 cup cashews

1 teaspoon onion powder
1/2 teaspoon garlic powder
1 teaspoon SWEETENER pg 6
1/2 teaspoon salt

Blend smooth all ingredients.

CARROT CHEESE SAUCE

Follow recipe for BASIC CHEESE SAUCE, page 28. To give an orange color, without pimento, use 2/3 cup cooked carrots. Add a small amount of additional water, if necessary, to blend.

CARROT CHEESE SPREAD

Follow the recipe for CHEESE SPREAD, page 27. Omit the pimento replacing it with 1/3 cup cooked carrots.

UN-TOMATO SOUP

2 cups soy milk
1 cup water
1 cup cooked carrots
3 tablespoons cooked beets
2 tablespoons cornstarch
2 teaspoons lemon juice

1/4 teaspoon basil
1/4 teaspoon garlic powder
1 1/2 teaspoons onion powder
1 1/4 teaspoons salt
1 teaspoon SWEETENER pg 6
1/16 teaspoon oregano

Blend smooth all but soy milk. Pour milk and blended portion into a sauce pan. Cook about 5-10 minutes, stirring until slightly thickened.

UN-TOMATO SPAGHETTI SAUCE

2 1/2 cups cooked carrots
1/3 cup cooked beets
1 cup water
2 tablespoons lemon juice
1 1/2 teaspoons salt
1 tablespoon cumin

1 teaspoon basil
1/2 teaspoon onion powder
1/8 teaspoon oregano
3/4 cup chopped onions
1 minced garlic clove

Cook onion and garlic in small amount of water. Blend all ingredients smooth.

UN-TOMATO PIZZA

Use the CARROT CHEESE SAUCE and UN-TOMATO SPAGHETTI SAUCE. May also use the SHREDDED TOFU CHEESE or SHREDDED AGAR CHEESE (leaving out the pimento). See PIZZA, page 56, in the Entree Section for remaining instructions concerning the crust and assembly of pizza.

UN-TOMATO LASAGNA

Use the CARROT CHEESE SAUCE and UN-TOMATO SPAGHETTI SAUCE, hot, double recipe. May want to also use the SHREDDED TOFU CHEESE or SHREDDED AGAR CHEESE (leaving out the pimento). Follow the instructions and remaining needed items from LASAGNA, page 57, in the Entree Section.

UN-TOMATO SPAGHETTI

Spaghetti, cooked. UN-TOMATO SPAGHETTI SAUCE, hot. CARROT CHEESE SAUCE and meatballs (meatballs may be made from PECAN LOAF, LOW-FAT PATTIES, TOFU PATTIES or OAT BURGERS). May want to also use the SHREDDED TOFU CHEESE or SHREDDED AGAR CHEESE (leaving out the pimento). Serve along with tossed salad, bread and spread.

CAULIFLOWER "POTATO" SALAD

See recipe for POTATO SALAD. Replace potatoes with chopped cauliflower steamed until tender/crisp.

UN-TOMATO CHILI

6 1/2 cups cooked salt free kidney beans

2 cups cooked carrots	**1 cup chopped, cooked onions**
1/2 cup cooked beets	**3 tablespoons lemon juice**
3 1/4 cups water or bean broth	**1 clove garlic**
4 teaspoons cumin	**1 teaspoon basil**
1 tablespoon salt	**1/2 teaspoon oregano**

1 1/2 tablespoons SWEETENER pg 6

Blend smooth all but beans and onion with 2 1/2 cups of the water, pour into a sauce pan. Rinse blender with remaining water, add to pan. Combine all ingredients. Cover and simmer until heated, stirring occasionally.

VARIATION: If using beans that already have salt added to them, then reduce the salt in the recipe to 1 teaspoon instead of 1 tablespoon.

FOOD DRYING

I began drying food in 1980 in my car. I started by stringing green beans with a needle and thread to make "leather britches". I also did some drying in an oven. Before long my brother, Mike, heard about what I was doing. Being the talented and wonderful brother that he is he built me a food dryer. He didn't mess around with a tabletop version. He built a six foot dryer that held alot of food! Wow, was I excited. I dried everything that grew on a tree, a bush, on a vine or in the garden. I still enjoy drying.

This section is not intended to take the place of a good book on how to dry fresh produce. It is really more to stimulate your imagination. This is a time to once again step into your laboratory, the kitchen, and feel the excitement of a new discovery. There are no failures in this lab, only learning. I am drying recipes from my cookbook. I started this when I wanted to pack food for my husband for canoe trips that he would take every year or two that would last for several days. Weight and space are issues when portaging a canoe and all your supplies around long, dangerous rapids through the woods and boughs. These recipes have proven to be useful in other situations besides camping, such as traveling or just for something quick and different. Plus, using dried food is a great way to save on food storage space and to use leftovers. You will find in this section recipes I have dried from my cookbook as well as items from the grocery store, such as apple sauce, olives, tofu and frozen veggies. I will go through each section of the cookbook discussing different recipes to dry.

BASIC DRYING INSTRUCTIONS

FILLING THE TRAYS

You will frequently find that when drying recipes, such as scalloped potatoes, chili or cheese sauces, they can not be placed directly on the average mesh drying tray without food dropping through the mesh. There are food dryer trays made for this purpose. The trays are a mesh but there is an additional solid, hard, plastic insert that can be laid over the mesh, especially designed for making fruit leather. This is very convenient. If this is not available then cover the tray with a layer of plastic wrap. Do not cover the ventilation hole if there is one in the middle of the tray. I like to first cover the tray from side to side with plastic wrap then use a sharp knife to slit the wrap at the vent hole then gently widen the wrap to fit snugly around the hole. This way takes a little longer but works just as well as the premade plastic trays. Generally when filling a tray do not fill it more than 1/4 inch thick. Sauces should only be about 1/8 inch thick. If drying individual pieces, such as tomato slices, frozen mixed vegetables or berries lay them in a single layer for best results. For the quickest,most even drying the trays should be rotated every 4 hours. When using plastic wrap it should be removed after a thick, sticky/dry film is formed on the top of the food. This is usually after about 6-8 hours. Do this by flipping the food over on the tray and peeling off the wrap. This will allow the food to dry more quickly to avoid spoilage. This can also be done if using a tray with the plastic inserts, it is not as necessary, but does help speed up the drying.

If you would like more information on a food dryer with plastic inserts you may contact me at the address in the front of this book.

DRYING TIME
This varies depending on the amount of water in the food, how thick the tray is covered with food, the size of the pieces and the humidity in the air. Most recipes take 12-24 hours to dry. Small, individual pieces, such as diced vegetables, just take a few hours if they are in a single layer. Do not add food during the drying process as this added moisture will retard the drying of the other foods and could cause spoilage. After some recipes are dried they can be crumble for easy storage. If the recipe is going to be blended into a powder then it is best to crumble the food for easy blending. If the food is in a sheet, like fruit leather, it can be stored as is or blended into a powder. Cut the sheet into pieces with scissors about one inch in diameter and use this way or blend to a grit like textured powder.

REHYDRATION
This varies significantly but is easy to adjust. I prefer to start with a minimum amount of water since the cooking time is a matter of minutes and it is easy to add water if desired. Most rehydrating of these recipes will be at a ratio of 1 part dry to 1 1/2 parts water. Sometimes the ratio is closer to 1:1. Sometimes the ratio is 1 part dry:2 1/2 parts water. Stir periodically during the cooking. The cooking time can be from 1-15 minutes. Sometimes it is only necessary to soak the food in water or just add boiling water and let sit 5 minutes. The point is there is room for experimenting. Some dishes will be at a good consistency at the time they are rehydrated, then they will thicken and need a small amount of water to thin them down by the next day. If too much water is added then more of the dried food can be added. Simply continue cooking until the added food is tender. Fruit or vegetable juice, bouillon, or leftover water from cooking vegetables can be used in place of water for rehydration.

STORAGE
To retain flavor and nutrients store dried food in glass out of direct light, in a cool place. Or store in the freezer in freezer bags. I have kept dried food for years but there is a gradual breakdown in nutritional and flavor quality.

DRIED BREAKFASTS

DRIED INSTANT CEREAL
Drying cooked cereals is a great way to save time and make your own instant cereal. Most whole grains need long, slow cooking to make them easier to digest and to get more nutritional value from the grains (see the WHOLE GRAIN COOKING CHART in the breakfast section).
Cover food dryer tray with plastic wrap. Spread cooked cereal on tray about 1/4 inch thick. Cereal will be hard and brittle when dry. To rehydrate: Place in sauce pan 1 part dried cereal and 1 1/2 parts water. Bring to a light boil, stirring occasionally, 5-10 minutes, until tender. Serve as desired.
Use same directions for CORN MILLET PORRIDGE & GLORIFIED RICE.

DRIED CHEESE AND MILK SUBSTITUTES

DRIED CHEESES
GOLDEN SAUCE, TENDER LOW-CAL CHEESE, BASIC CHEESE SAUCE and CHEESE SPREAD can all be successfully dried with very good results. They rehydrate just like when freshly made. These cheeses become more versatile because in their dried form they may be added to foods as a seasoning, such as soups, beans or quiche, without affecting the consistency of the dish. They may be sprinkled on salads, over dishes such as tacos, pizza or scalloped potatoes or on popcorn. They may be stirred into salad dressing, mayonnaise, a spread or gravy. The cheese sauces may be used as a crisp cracker once they are dried. When doing this cut the salt in the recipe at least in half. This is a nice chip substitute for those with certain grain allergies. Cheese not to dry is the TOFU CHEESE SAUCE. Recipes using Mori-Nu Tofu will not soften and return to a nice consistency. Any of the other cheese variations may be used.

Prepare the recipe according to the directions then spread over a tray covered with plastic wrap. Dry until crisp. At this time crumble the pieces or blend to a powder and store.

REHYDRATING CHEESES
Rehydrating can be done in different ways such as:
1-Soak 1 part powdered cheese in 1 1/2 parts water for an hour.
2-Soak 1 part powdered cheese in 1 1/2 parts boiling water several minutes.
As stated in methods 1 & 2 begin with a ratio of 1:1 1/2. You will probably increase to 2 parts water but starting out with less is best.
3-My favorite way is the lightly boil 1 part powdered cheese to 2 parts water for 3-5 minutes, blend smooth then chill. This brief cooking seems to

make cheese the thickest. That is why I start with 2 cups of water instead of 1 1/2 cups as in methods 1 and 2.

After all these methods it is necessary to blend the cheese if you desire to make it smooth like the original recipe. Chilling will thicken the sauce.

If the dried cheese is left in small pieces and not powdered then start with 1 part pieces of cheese to 1 part water and follow one of the methods just explained. GOLDEN SAUCE usually takes closer to 2 1/2 parts water.

DRIED AGAR CHEESE

Cut the salt in the original recipe in half if making to eat in the dried state. Cut the cheese into slices then lay onto mesh tray. Eat it in chunks as is, or drop in soup, or soak the slices for several minutes in equal amount of water to slices. Cheese will not rehydrate like the original recipe but is still tasty. Drying the SHREDDED AGAR CHEESE works very well. After the grated cheese is dried place it in a tall, narrow container. Fill with water to the top of the cheese and let it soak 30-60 minutes. It will retain its grated shape and is good for recipes where a grated cheese is desired. Cheese will not melt.

DRIED DESSERTS

Prepare the following recipes according to directions then spread over a drying tray that is covered with plastic wrap and dry until crisp. Blend recipe to a powder. Use 1 part powder to 1 1/2 parts water. More water may be added according to desired consistency. (If recipe is not powdered then less water will be needed. Approximately 1:1) Note the rehydrating directions under the cheese recipes for how to prepare the following recipes. MILLET PUDDING (do not use the variation using Mori-Nu Tofu), CREAMY LOW-CAL TOPPING, COCONUT FROSTING, CAROB PEANUT BUTTER FROSTING.

DRIED DRESSINGS, GRAVIES & SPREADS

Prepare the following recipes according to directions then spread over a drying tray that is covered with plastic wrap and dry until crisp. Blend recipe to a powder. Use 1 part powder to 1 1/2 parts water. More water may be added according to desired consistency. (If recipe is not powdered then less water will be needed. Approximately 1:1) Note the rehydrating directions under the cheese recipes for how to prepare the following recipes. SUN SEED TOMATO DRESSING, HUMMUS, LOW-CAL FRENCH DRESSING (not made with tofu), QUICK CORN SAUCE, CREAMY LOW-CAL MAYONNAISE, SUN SEED SPREAD, YEASTY SPREAD, BEAN SPREAD, KETCHUP, MILLET BUTTER, FRESH CORN BUTTER, CAROB

MILLET SAUCE, APPLE BUTTER, FRUIT SPREAD, STRAWBERRY JAM
Recipes with a large amount of oil, such as the FRENCH TOMATO DRESS-
ING, do not dry well.

DRIED GRAVY

With the gravy recipes in this cookbook blend smooth all the ingredients
except the additional water. Spread over a tray covered with plastic wrap.
Dry until crisp. Blend to a powder. One recipe will make about 2/3 cup dry
powder. When rehydrating start with 2/3 cup powder and blend it with 1
cup of water. If this step is skipped then the gravy will be more grainy.
Empty blender into sauce pan. Rinse blender with 2 cups of water and
pour into pan. Bring to a boil, stirring, until thickened. More water may be
desired but probably less than 1 cup. The original recipe in the cookbook
calls for 4 cups of additional water but this seems to make it too runny.

DRIED ENTREES

DRIED MISCELLANEOUS AND BEAN ENTREES

Prepare the following recipes according to directions, including the cook-
ing or baking, spread finished product over a drying tray that is covered
with plastic wrap. When dry crumble into small pieces but do not blend.
Use 1 part dry ingredients to 1 1/2 parts water. Lightly boil until tender.
When rehydrating beans or a dish with beans in it, such as Spanish Rice,
the cooking is longer, usually about 12 minutes, stirring occasionally.
MILLET TOMATO LOAF, SPANISH RICE, EASY BEANS, SAVORY BEANS
& RICE, BAKED BEANS, CHICKPEA A LA KING.

DRIED SCRAMBLED TOFU

This may be dried if using water packed tofu (Mori-Nu Tofu is like very
tough rubber when dried). Prepare the recipe then dry on a tray covered
with plastic wrap. When dry crumble into small pieces but do not blend. To
rehydrate lightly boil 1 part tofu to 1 1/2 parts water 12 minutes, stirring
occasionally. Add more water if needed. The texture will remain chewy. It is
good stirred with a spread or mayonnaise for a sandwich or added to a
salad or into a soup. The recipe may also be blended after it is dried. Add
it to powdered spaghetti sauce and powdered beans or a loaf to make a
sandwich spread. See DRIED SANDWICH SPREAD in this section.
NOTE OF INTEREST: 4 pounds (or about 8 cups, mashed) of tofu makes
about 5 cups of dried, crumbled tofu and 2 1/2 cups of powdered tofu.

DRIED BAKED OR CHIPPED TOFU

This may be dried if using water packed tofu (Mori-Nu Tofu is like very
tough rubber when dried). Prepare the recipe as directed then dry directly

on a mesh drying tray. Tofu should be in bite size pieces before drying. This is tasty added to soups or stews. The tofu should lightly boil for 12-15 minutes to soften. It can also be added to a moist casserole with gravy or a pot pie that will be baked at least 45 minutes. Or add pieces to gravy on the stove and boil until softened. Tofu will always remain chewy.

OR try partially drying tofu for chewy, moist texture. Store in refrigerator.

DRIED SPAGHETTI SAUCE

Dry on a tray covered with plastic wrap until like leather. Cut into small pieces and blend. 11 1/2 cups cooked sauce dehydrates to 2 2/3 cups powdered. Use 1 part powder to 2 1/2 cups water. Lightly boil 3 minutes or just add boiling water to sauce and let sit 30-60 minutes until thickened.

DRIED LOAVES AND PATTIES

These may also be dried but they will not return to their freshly made condition. Regardless, they are still useful, tasty and worth drying. Prepare PECAN LOAF, LOW-FAT PATTIES, TOFU LOAF (made with water packed tofu), QUICK BEAN PATTIES, OATBURGERS, GARBANZO RICE PATTIES, TOFU PATTIES (made with water packed tofu) according to directions, including baking. These can be dried directly on a mesh drying tray. Slice loaf into 1/4 inch slices. Patties should be broken into 3 or 4 pieces. Put food side by side, in a single layer. Will be brittle when dry. Blend or crumble into small pieces. The dried loaves and patties, blended to a powder, make delicious sandwich spreads. See recipe in this section. Small, crumbled pieces may be added to soups or stews but they will not retain their shape once in the liquid. They may also be added to sauce when making lasagna or pizza.

DRIED SCALLOPED POTATOES

These are yummmy when rehydated. Prepare the recipe according to the directions, including baking. Dry on a tray covered with plastic wrap. Will be hard and brittle when dry. Add 1 part potatoes to 1 1/4 parts water. Lightly boil, stirring occasionally, 12-15 minutes. Add more water if needed. Potatoes will remain a little chewy. Dried potatoes may also be blended to a powder and added to soups or stews.

DRIED NIGHTSHADES

Prepare the following recipes according to directions then spread over a drying tray that is covered with plastic wrap, dry until brittle or hard. After drying the recipes should be blended to a powder. Mix 1 part powder with 1 1/2 parts water. More water may be added according to desired consistency. (If they are not powdered then less water will be needed. Approxi-

mately 1:1) Note the rehydrating directions under the cheese recipes for how to rehydrate the following recipes:
UN-TOMATO KETCHUP, UN-FRENCH DRESSING, CARROT CHEESE SAUCE, CARROT CHEESE SPREAD, UN-TOMATO CHILI, UN-TOMATO SPAGHETTI SAUCE.
For UN-TOMATO SOUP: Begin with 1 part powder to 2 1/2 parts water.

DRIED SALADS, SOUPS & VEGETABLES

DRIED MISCELLANEOUS SOUPS

Prepare the following recipes according to directions then spread over a drying tray that is covered with plastic wrap, dry until crisp or hard. Crumble into small pieces. These should not be blended. CHILI, LIMA BEAN CHOWDER, BROCCOLI CHEESE SOUP, SPLIT PEA CHOWDER. To rehydrate lightly boil in water 10-15 minutes, stirring occasionally. Begin with 1 part recipe to 1 1/2 parts water. Some of these will require more water such as Split Pea Chowder, it will be closer to 2 1/2 parts water.

DRIED CREAM OF TOMATO SOUP

This recipe should be powdered. Use 1 part dry to 3 parts water. SPLIT PEA CHOWDER may also be powdered. Use 1 part dry to 3 parts water. Both of these take 2-3 minutes of cooking. Add more water if needed. Leave covered in sauce pan and let sit 5 minutes to thicken.

ADDITIONAL FOOD DRYING IDEAS

DRIED VEGETABLES

Dry any frozen or canned vegetables. Spread out on tray in a single layer. If it looks like the food may drop through the mesh tray while shrinking then dry on plastic wrap. Vegetables may be left in the size pieces they were dried in or they may be blended to a powder. The pieces will take anywhere from a few minutes to soften in lightly boiling water to 15 minutes. Always use a covered sauce pan. The powder may be added to a variety of dishes, such as, gravies, soups, dressings, cheese sauce, breads, cookies, beans, casseroles, burgers, loaves, or sprinkled on salads.

DRIED ZUCCHINI

This is a very good way to use excess garden zucchini. Shred then dry. No precooking needed. May want to stir in CHICKEN STYLE SEASONING before placing on mesh drying trays. To rehydrate add 1 part dry to 1 part water. Lightly boil 3-5 minutes adding more water if needed. May also add dried to bread to make ZUCCHINI BREAD. Use less dried than if using fresh zucchini. May need to add up to 3/4 cup of water back to recipe.

D PIMENTO

ried pimento in place of canned pimento in recipes where it is used
:es for color or in cheese sauce. This can be a money saver if buying
ito in large cans then drying. OR buy sweet red peppers by the bushel
ison from a produce market, or grow your own, chop up and dry. No
hing is needed as with some vegetables. 3 cups canned pimento at a
it of 28 ounces equal 1 3/4 cups dried flakes at a weight of 1 1/2
es! Flakes may be blended in the blender to make a powder at this
if desired. This really saves on storage space. Add 3 tablespoons of
pimento flakes or 2 teaspoons ground pimento when making BASIC
:ESE SAUCE on page 29.

IED OLIVES

e and dry. 5 cups canned olives dehydrates to 2 cups. They are very
tender. Rehydation is optional. Add to salad or any dish using olives. Just
remember they are very salty in dried state so use sparingly.

DRIED LEFTOVERS

Most any leftover may be dried. It's a great way to save on food waste.

DRIED APPLE SAUCE

Pour apple sauce, or any other fruit sauce, onto mesh tray covered with
plastic wrap. Dry until like leather. Cut into pieces with scissors and use or
blend into a powder. If rehydrating from powder use the following directions: 1 part powder to 2 1/2 parts liquid (water or fruit juice). Sauce may
be prepared two different ways. (1) Quick way: Lightly boil in a covered
sauce pan 5 minutes then let sit 5 minutes. (2) Easy way: Put powdered
sauce and liquid in a container and let soak one hour.

DRIED CHIPS

Cut the salt in half in MILLET BUTTER or BASIC CHEESE SAUCE. Spread
over tray covered with plastic wrap. When partially dry, after 4-6 hours,
score into desired shapes for chips and finish drying.

DRIED SANDWICH SPREAD

Mix equal amounts of blended dried tomato or spaghetti sauce and/or
dried cheese sauce with twice as much dried blended loaf or patty. May
also use cooked beans that have been dried and blended. Lightly boil 3
minutes 1 part dry ingredients with 2 parts water in a covered sauce pan.
Remove from heat and let sit 2 minutes then serve.
Ways to serve: As a sandwich spread, a filling in ROLL UPS, tortillas or
enchiladas, on pizza or in lasagna, in STUFFED PEPPERS OR ZUCCHINI
OR CABBAGE ROLLS added to SCRAMBLED TOFU.

SALADS, SOUPS & VEGETABLES

In all food preparation it is desirable to make individual dishes simple, and to serve few dishes at a meal. Care should be used that salads are not complex mixtures. If part of the cooked food for the meal is made from carrots, cabbage, celery, greens or tomato, use these same items as a part of the salad.

Use one to three vegetables together depending on how many varieties are being cooked. Be artistic, using a variety of methods for preparation such as slicing, dicing and shredding. Invest in garnishing tools.

SPROUTS

Sprouts are very economical and highly nutritious. Sprout seeds, beans and grains. Almost any whole natural seed may be sprouted. Be sure to buy untreated seeds. They may be obtained where health foods are sold.

1. When using a 1 quart jar add: 2 tablespoons of alfalfa seeds; 3 tablespoons of broccoli, radish, cabbage or red clover seed (or mix alfalfa with these seeds); 1/4 cup mung beans; 1/2 cup unhulled grains, such as whole grain wheat berries; 1 cup of peas or beans. Put seeds, grain or beans in quart jar. Cover with 3 times as much water. Soak 8-12 hours. Grains, beans and peas are generally best when sprouts are 1/2-3/4 inches long. Most sprouts take 4-5 days. Many beans may grow 1-1 1/2 inches. Alfalfa, radish and other small seeds may also grow 1-1 1/2 inches and be tasty.

2. Secure a piece of fiberglass mesh, hardware cloth or other permeable material (not aluminum treated window screen) over the top of the jar. Use a jar ring or cut the middle out of a lid and screw on over the screen. Cheese cloth or nylon stockings will work but are not as easy to use during the rinsing stage. Sprouting tops may be purchased in health food stores.

3. Pour off water used for the initial soaking. Add more water to rinse seeds then invert jar for several minutes in a dish drainer or bowl to thoroughly drain. Rinse twice daily. Some beans spoil easily and should be rinsed 3 to 5 times daily in hot weather. Always drain sprouts well.

4. After bean or grain sprouts have reached desired length rinse one final time. Drain well on a paper towel then refrigerate in closed container. With alfalfa, radish and other small seeds place them in a bowl. Cover with water and gently swish in a circular motion. Most of the brown hulls will float to the rim or sink to the bottom. Scoop out the ones on top. Don't try

to get them all! Drain well on paper towel or in a vegetable spinner. Refrigerate in closed container. Removing hulls is optional.

5. Cooking- Seeds and grains, sprouted, may be eaten raw. Beans and peas will be more digestible, therefore more nutritious, if allowed to steam 15-20 minutes.

POTATO SALAD

2 cups cooked, cubed potatoes
1 cup finely diced celery
1/4-1/2 cup diced onions
1/4-1/2 cup sliced olives
1 1/2 cups TOFU MAYONNAISE

1 tablespoon lemon juice
1 teaspoon onion powder
1/4 teaspoon salt
2 tablespoons chopped parsley
   OR 1 tablespoon dried parsley

Stir all ingredients together. Chill several hours.

THREE BEAN SALAD

1 15.5 oz. can kidney beans, drained
1 15.5 oz. can garbanzo beans, drained
1 15.5 oz. can green or waxed beans or a combination, drained
1/4 cup diced onion
   OR 1/2 cup chopped celery
3/4 cup sliced olives
1/4 cup lemon juice
3 tablespoons SWEETENER pg 6

1/4 teaspoon garlic powder
3/4 teaspoon salt
2 tablespoons diced pimento
1/2 teaspoon onion powder
1/4 cup water

Stir vegetables and olives together. Combine lemon juice, water and seasonings together. Mix all together well. Chill several hours to blend flavors. Yield 5 cups.

FRUIT SOUP

3 cups pineapple juice
3 cups apple juice
1/2 cup granulated tapioca
1 20 oz. can pineapple, chunks or crushed

1 cup chopped dried fruit
2-3 sliced bananas
2 cups additional chopped fruit

Combine tapioca and juice. Lightly boil, stirring, until tapioca is clear. Add remaining ingredients. Chill. Any of the juices or fruits may be changed based on preferences.

CHILI

2 cups dry kidney beans
8 1/2 cups water
1 6 oz. can tomato paste
2 14 oz. cans diced tomatoes
1 cup chopped onion
3/4 cup chopped green pepper

2 chopped garlic cloves
2 tablespoons cumin
2 teaspoons onion powder
1 1/2 teaspoon basil
3/4 teaspoon oregano
2 1/2 teaspoons salt

Soak 2 cups dry beans in 6 cups of water 6-8 hours. Drain beans; do not save water. Lightly boil beans and the 8 1/2 cups of water in a covered pan until beans are soft, about 2 1/2 hours, stir occasionally. Add vegetables and continue cooking 20 minutes. Add seasonings, cook 10 more minutes.

LIMA BEAN CHOWDER

1 1/2 cups frozen lima beans
1 cup chopped onion
2 1/2 cups cooked, diced potatoes
3/4 cup corn

1 chopped garlic clove
1/3 cup white flour
1 3/4 teaspoons salt
4 cups soy milk

Dice potatoes after cooking. Cook remaining vegetables until tender. Lightly boil milk and flour together until thickened. Mix all together and reheat.

VARIATION: Replace soy milk with 3/4 cup of cashews, 3 3/4 cups water and 1/4 teaspoon salt. Blend smooth nuts with 1 cup of the water, rinse blender with remaining water and add to pan with salt. Cut flour to 1/4 cup.

BROCCOLI CHEESE SOUP

1 1/4 cups cooked potato
1 1/2 cups cooked carrots
1 medium cooked onion
1 pound frozen broccoli or 4 cups fresh, chopped

3 1/4 cups water
1 3/4 teaspoons salt
1/2 cup cashews

Cook broccoli until tender. Blend potatoes and cashews with 2 cups of the water. Blend carrots and onion with the remaining 1 1/4 cup water. Combine all ingredients. Reheat and serve. Sliced, cooked carrots may be used for part of broccoli. Serve with tossed salad that has chopped, fresh broccoli in it that has been steamed or blanched a few minutes then chilled.

VARIATION: Reduce cashews to 1/4 cup, leave out broccoli. Serve as sauce over noodles, rice, potatoes or vegetables.

CREAM OF TOMATO SOUP

2 cups soy milk
4 cups canned tomatoes
1 1/2 teaspoons onion powder
3/4 teaspoon salt
1 1/2 teaspoons SWEETENER pg 6

1/3 cup flour
1/4 teaspoon garlic powder
1/4 teaspoon basil
1/8 teaspoon oregano

Blend tomatoes and dry ingredients until smooth. Mix all ingredients. Lightly boil, stirring often, until thickened.

VARIATION: Replace soy milk with 1/3 cup cashews and 1 3/4 cups water. Blend smooth nuts with 1/2 cup water, add remaining water and reblend.

SPLIT PEA CHOWDER

6 cups water
1/2 cup brown rice
1 cup dry split peas
1 cup chopped onions

1 cup diced carrots
1 cup diced celery
2 teaspoons salt
1 teaspoon basil

Lightly boil rice and peas in a covered pan 1 1/2 hours. Add vegetables and continue to cook 20 minutes. Add seasonings and cook an additional 5 minutes. Chowder is thicker next day.

CHICKEN NOODLE SOUP

1 15.5 oz. can garbanzo beans, drained or 1 1/2 cups cooked beans
2 tablespoons CHICKEN STYLE SEASONING pg 63
5 1/2 cups water
1 1/2 cups uncooked noodle flats
1 chopped onion

2 bay leaves
2 tablespoons dry parsley flakes
1/4 teaspoon salt

Combine all ingredients and lightly boil about 15 minutes, until onions and noodles are cooked.

VEGETABLES

There are many different ways to make vegetables taste well seasoned without over using salt or oil, as well as avoiding harmful substances such as vinegar, pepper and other undesirable spices.

Delicious and quick: Add 1 tablespoon of CHICKEN STYLE SEASON-ING, page 63, while cooking, to approximately 4 cups cooked vegetables. OR sprinkle TASTY SESAME TOPPING on cooked vegetables or salads. OR several of the dressings and spreads (i.e., SUN SEED SPREAD, SUN SEED TOMATO DRESSING, MILLET BUTTER, FRESH CORN BUTTER, CHEESE SPREAD, BASIC CHEESE SAUCE) make vegetables new and interesting. GOLDEN SAUCE over broccoli or carrots is delicious.

Steaming in a pan with a tight fitting lid helps preserve nutrients. Whether boiling or steaming save leftover cooking water. This water may contain 50% or more of the water soluble nutrients from the food. Use the water to cook more vegetables, dried beans or whole grains, or to make gravy, soup, patties, a loaf, dressing, bread, waffles or crackers.

SAUTEING VEGETABLES WITHOUT OIL

Place a small amount of water in a sauce pan. Add chopped vegetables, cover and cook on low or medium heat until tender. Stir as needed. Extra water may be needed while cooking.

GREEN BEAN CASSEROLE

Place cooked beans in casserole dish. Pour gravy of choice over beans and top with bread or cracker crumbs, or CROUTONS. Bake until hot.

DILLY GREEN BEANS

2 cups cooked green beans, carrots or mixed vegetables
1/2 cup chopped onions　　　　**1/4 cup water**
1 chopped garlic clove　　　　**salt to taste**
1/2 teaspoon dill weed

Cook onion and garlic in the 1/4 cup of water. When tender add vegetables and seasoning. Heat and serve. Dill is an herb which tastes good with many vegetables.

SIMPLY DELICIOUS VEGIES

Stir CHICKEN STYLE SEASONING, page 63, into vegetables of choice while cooking. Use 1 tablespoon for approximately 4 cups cooked veg-etables. Add seasoning during the last 3-5 minutes of cooking. It is best to stir in if vegetables are cooking in a small amount of water so that much of the seasoning isn't left in the cooking water.

STEAMED CABBAGE

4 cups chopped cabbage　　　　**1/2 teaspoon caraway seed**
1/4 cup water
2 teaspoons CHICKEN STYLE SEASONING pg 63

Add ingredients to boiling water. Cover. Steam 10 minutes, until tender.

VARIATIONS:
1. Replace half of cabbage with shredded carrots.
2. Substitute shredded turnips or rutabaga for cabbage. Steam a few minutes longer. May need to add more water. Stir occasionally.

EGGPLANT OR ZUCCHINI STACKS

large zucchini or peeled eggplant　　**onion slices**
tomato slices　　　　　　　　　　　**green pepper slices**
CHEESE SAUCE or GOLDEN SAUCE or TENDER LOW-CAL CHEESE

Slice zucchini or eggplant in 3/8" slices, allowing 2-4 good-sized slices per person. If using eggplant, soak slices in salted water for 15 minutes (1 1/2 teaspoons salt per 4 cups water). This step is optional but it seems to help eliminate the slightly harsh or bitter taste that is characteristic of eggplant. Drain slices and place on oiled cookie sheet, sprinkle with salt if did not soak in salt water. Place a slice of tomato on each eggplant or zucchini, sprinkle a few grains of salt, and a slice of onion and green pepper followed with a few grains of salt. Bake at 350 degrees for 30 minutes. Remove from oven and top each stack with as much cheese as desired. (Cheese will be thicker and more will stay on each stack if the cheese is chilled before using.) Bake additional 20 minutes or until vegetables are tender when pierced.

ZUCCHINI, CORN AND TOMATOES

2 medium size zucchini, about 2 lbs. or 4 cups sliced
2 1/2 cups canned tomatoes　　　**1 1/2 teaspoons salt**
1 1/2 cups corn　　　　　　　　　**3/4 teaspoon basil**
1/2 cup thinly sliced onion　　　　**1/2 teaspoon oregano**

Slice zucchini on diagonal. Combine all ingredients. Simmer until tender. Serve as is or over brown rice, potatoes or noodles. Vary the vegetables. Try summer squash, broccoli, carrots, okra or green beans instead of zucchini. Add water for cooking if needed.

HOW MUCH FAT DO I WANT TO EAT?

How much fat do you want to eat in a day? Many are trying to limit their intake to around 20% of their calories in fat for better health. But how can you easily figure what that means? For most men 1800-2800 calories per day is sufficient. For most women 1200-2000 is enough. The following exercise will show how to figure what 20% looks like.

Total calories consumed in one day is 2000. 20% of this is 400 calories. There are about 40 calories in one teaspoon of fat. 400 ÷ 40 = 10 teaspoons of fat for the day. There are 9 calories per gram of fat so 400 ÷ = -0\] 9 = 44 grams.

Therefore: 2000 total calories per day
400 calories in fat at 20% or
10 teaspoons of fat or
44 grams

HOW TO READ A LABEL

The following guide will show how to change grams and milligrams into teaspoons. This is an easy, visual way for many to judge what they are eating. Protein and carbohydrates both have **4 calories per gram**. This is the same regardless if the protein is from plant or animal. Complex and simple carbohydrates both have 4 calories per gram. Fats, whether animal or vegetable, are more concentrated and have **9 calories per gram**.

Here is a simple exercise to use when reading labels.

FATS
Lets take a 1.8 oz. package of two small Reeses Peanut Butter Cups. This contains 17 grams of fat. This is on the label. 17 grams x 9 calories per gram = 153. There are 153 calories of fat in the candy. Now, in order to find how many teaspoons this represents one has to know that in fat there is approximately 40 calories per teaspoon. Therefore 153 ÷ 40 = 3.83, or nearly 4 teaspoons of fat.

SUGAR
Reeses, like many candies, cereals and other products, divides the carbohydrates into "simple" and "complex". There are 24 grams of simple carbohydrates, or sugars, in this small 1.8 oz. package as stated on the label. 24 grams x 4 calories per gram = 96 calories of sugar. Sugar has 15 calories per teaspoon. Therefore, 96 ÷ 15 = 6.4 or 6 ½ teaspoons of sugar. The average American eats 46 teaspoons of sugar daily.

SODIUM

Most people in good health should not exceed 1 teaspoon of salt per day. 1 teaspoon of salt = 2200 mg of sodium. Labels are written in milligrams (mg). If the label says on a can of condensed tomato soup that there are 760mg of sodium in a 1 cup serving that is mixed half and half with water, then 760 ÷ 2200 = .35 or 35%. 35% of a teaspoon is 1/3 teaspoon of salt or 1/3 of the entire day's recommendation in one cup of soup!

INSTRUCTIONS ON EATING

The disease and suffering that everywhere prevail are largely due to popular errors in regard to diet. What we eat and drink today, walks and talks tomorrow. By carefully heeding the following instructions you may avoid many illnesses:

1. Eat largely of fruits, grains, and vegetables prepared in a natural yet tasty way. Limit rich foods, keeping sugars to 3 teaspoons, salt to 1 teaspoon, and oil to 2 tablespoons daily. Fruit juices and other concentrated foods usually should be taken in small quantities.

2. Vary your diet from meal to meal but do not eat too many varieties at any one meal. A main dish, along with an additional cooked and raw dish plus bread with a spread and/or dressing is a plan that may be helpful.

3. Use more of the whole grains and less food prepared from refined grains. Cooked cereals are generally better than dry cereals unless using a cereal made with little or no honey, sugar or oil.

4. Eat at the same mealtime daily and allow at least 5 hours from the end of one meal to the beginning of the next. This includes any items with caloric value such as juice, mints, chewing gum, fruits, etc., as they will delay the digestion of food already in the stomach from the previous meal.

5. Eat a substantial breakfast that should more nearly correspond to the largest meal of the day. Eat only a light supper, fruit and whole grains, (such as an apple and a few crackers without butter), and this two or three hours or more before retiring so that the stomach may also rest.

6. Eat all you need to maintain health, and enjoy your food, but don't overeat. Too much food dulls and depresses the mind, causing disease and fatigue and shortens life.

7. Eating slowly and chewing your food thoroughly will increase the enjoyment as well as the nutritional benefits derived from it.

8. Drink enough water daily to keep the urine quite pale, but do not drink with your meals or immediately before or after them as this will delay digestion.

9. The following are a list of what are harmful foods. Total abstinence is recommended: spices such as hot pepper (black or red), ginger, cinnamon, cloves, nutmeg, mustard and horseradish. These are items that in their cold state are hot to the tongue. Also baking powder and soda, vinegar, spoiled, aged or fermented foods including ketchup, mayonnaise, ripened (or hard) cheese. Also pressed or ground meats, rare, treated or aged meats. All of these will irritate the gastrointestinal tract, particularly the stomach, can cause fermentation, noticeable by gas and will create a burden on the digestive system. Combinations of large quantities of milk and sugar, with or without eggs, such as in custards, ice cream, sherbets and cakes or combining fruits and vegetables in the same meal lead to fermentation in the stomach and eventually weakening the system. Coffee, tea, chocolate and some soft drinks contain caffeine or similar substances that have many harmful effects including: aids in the production of ulcers, raises the blood pressure, increases the heart rate, aggravates hypoglycemia and diabetes, contributes to coronary heart disease, increases risk of stomach and bladder cancer, crosses the placenta and affects the unborn child and is an addictive drug.

CHEESE

A summary of the objectionable features of hard or ripened cheeses includes the following:

1. The putrefactive process, which cheese undergoes, results in the production of amines, ammonia, irritating fatty acids (butyric, caproic, caprylic, etc.). The carbohydrate is converted to lactic acid. These are all waste products that cause irritation to nerves and the gastrointestinal tract.

2. Migraine headaches can be caused by tyramine, one of the toxic amines produced in cheese.

3. Certain of the amines can interact with the nitrates present in the stomach to form nitrosamine, a cancer producing agent.

4. An intolerance to lactose, the chief carbohydrate of cheese and milk, is probably the most common food sensitivity in America.

5. Rennet is used in cheese making. It comes from the stomach of calves, lambs or pigs.

EATING BETWEEN MEALS

X-ray studies conducted to determine the emptying time of the normal stomach shows the average to be between four and five hours. A study was run using several persons who were given a routine breakfast consisting of cereal and cream, bread, cooked fruit and an egg. Their stomachs were x-rayed and found to be empty in four and one-half hours.

A few days later these same persons were given the same type of breakfast and two hours later they were fed snacks, their emptying time was checked. The results are as follows:

NORMAL BREAKFAST	TWO HOURS LATER	RESULTS
Person No. 1	Ice cream cone	Residue in the stomach after 6 hours
Person No. 2	Peanut butter sandwich	Residue after 9 hours
Person No. 3	Pumpkin pie, glass of milk	Residue after 9 hours
Person No. 4	Half slice of bread and butter repeated every one and one-half hour interval and no dinner	More than half of breakfast in stomach after 9 hours
Person No. 5	Twice in the morning and twice in the afternoon a bit of chocolate candy	Thirteen and one half hours later more than one-half the morning meal was still in the stomach

85

SUGAR ANDTHE BODY

The average American consumes 46 teaspoons of sugar each day. Most people are unaware of the amounts of sugar in ordinary pastries, desserts, drinks, and snack foods. An important fact about sugar has to do with disease resistance. Our white blood cells destroy bacteria. However, when the blood sugar level goes up these cells get sluggish. Think of the significance of the following chart when you consider that there are 60 to 400 trillion phagocytic white blood cells active in the human body.

EFFECT OF SUGAR INTAKE ON ABILITY OF
WHITE BLOOD CELLS TO DESTROY BACTERIA

Teaspoons of sugar eaten at one time by average adult	Number of bacteria destroyed by each WBC in 30 minutes	Percentage decrease in ability to destroy bacteria
0	14	0
6	10	25
12	5.5	60
18	2	85
24	1	92
uncontrolled diabetic	1	92

NOTES

NOTES

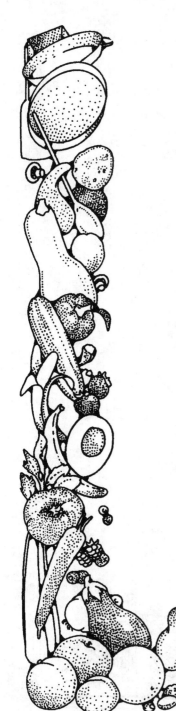

NOTES

NOTES

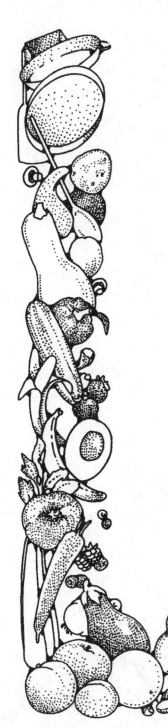

Index

Recipes Using Soy

(with some of these recipes the soy is used in a variation under the recipe)

MORE BOOKS FROM
FAMILY HEALTH PUBLICATIONS

OF THESE YE MAY FREELY EAT JoAnn Rachor --- 2.95
THE COUNTRY LIFE VEGETARIAN COOKBOOK Diana Fleming --------------------- 9.95
TASTE & SEE: ALLERGY RELIEF COOKING Penny King --------------------------------- 11.95
COUNTRY KITCHEN COLLECTION Silver Hills Institute --------------------------------- 11.95
100% VEGETARIAN: EATING NATURALLY FROM
YOUR GROCERY STORE Julianne Pickle --- 6.95
NEW START LIFESTYLE COOKBOOK Weimar Institute ----------------------------------- 19.99
BEST GOURMET RECIPES Five Loaves Deli and Bakery --------------------------------- 15.95
THE BEST OF SILVER HILLS Eileen & Debbie Brewer ------------------------------------ 11.95
COOKING BY THE BOOK Marcella Lynch --- 14.99
COOKING WITH NATURAL FOODS Muriel Beltz --- 14.95
COOKING WITH NATURAL FOODS II Muriel Beltz --- 14.95
EAT FOR STRENGTH (Oil Free Edition) Agatha Thrash, MD ------------------------- 8.95
ABSOLUTELY VEGETARIAN Lorine Tadej -- 8.95
TOFU COOKERY Louise Hagler --- 15.95
TOFU: QUICK AND EASY Louise Hagler --- 8.95
NUTRITION FOR VEGETARIANS Agatha & Calvin Thrash, MD ------------------------ 14.95
NATURAL HEALTH CARE FOR YOUR CHILD Phylis Austin, Thrash & Thrash ----- 9.95
HOME REMEDIES Agatha & Calvin Thrash, MD --- 14.95
NATURAL REMEDIES Austin, Thrash & Thrash, MD -------------------------------------- 6.95
MORE NATURAL REMEDIES Austin, Thrash & Thrash, MD ------------------------------ 6.95
FOOD ALLERGIES MADE SIMPLE Austin, Thrash & Thrash, MD --------------------- 4.95
PRESCRIPTION:CHARCOAL Agatha & Calvin Thrash, MD ------------------------------ 6.95
FATIGUE:CAUSES, TREATMENT AND PREVENTION Austin, Thrash & Thrash --- 4.95
ANIMAL CONNECTION Agatha & Calvin Thrash, MD --------------------------------------- 6.95
DIABETES & THE HYPOGLYCEMIC SYND Agatha & Calvin Thrash, MD ----------- 14.95
NATURAL TREATMENTS FOR HYPERTENSION Agatha & Calvin Thrash, MD---- 14.95
POISON WITH A CAPITAL C Agatha & Calvin Thrash, MD ------------------------------- 3.00
PROOF POSITIVE Neil Nedley, MD --- 49.00
EATING FOR GOOD HEALTH Winston Craig, PhD --- 9.95
THE USE & SAFETY OF COMMON HERBS & HERBAL TEAS Winston Craig ---- 8.95
MOOOOVE OVER MILK Vicki Griffin, PhD -- 9.99
NEW START Vernon Foster, MD -- 13.95
DON'T DRINK YOUR MILK Frank Osld, MD -- 7.95
DIET FOR ALL REASONS (Video) Michael Klaper, MD-------------------------------------- 21.95
YOU CAN'T IMPROVE ON GOD (Video) Lorraine Day, MD ------------------------------- 19.95

Please attach name and address
and phone number.

Subtotal _____

MI residents add
6% sales tax_____

Remit check to:
Family Health Publications L.L.C.
8777 E. Musgrove Hwy.
Sunfield MI 48890

Shipping:
$2.75 1st book
.75 each addl._____

Total Amount Closed_____